Secrets and Keys

Publisher Information

Published by Mervin Telford

Copyright © 2014 Mervin Telford

All rights reserved. No part of this publication may be reproduced, stored in a retrieval system, or transmitted in any form or by any means, electronic, mechanical, photocopying, recording or otherwise, without the prior permission of the author.

This is a work of fiction. Names, characters, places, and incidents are products of the author's imagination or are used fictitiously and should not be construed as real. Any resemblance to actual events, locales, organisations or persons, living or dead, is entirely coincidental.

Contact the author: elixirpoetry@gmail.com

ISBN: 978-0-9929544-3-7

Secrets and Keys

Mervin Telford

I dedicate this book to my children and family.

I also lovingly dedicate these poems to my global brothers and sisters of all colours, creeds and beliefs.

Through trial and error we have come a long way. I believe we will go so much further when through trial and realisation we become one benevolent mind within a seamless expanse of harmonic interactions.

Then we will have paradise on earth for all of humanity.

Secrets and Keys

AN ODE TO LOVE	1
JEALOUSY'S BEAST	5
THE STRONG PLACE	8
TEARS AND FIRE	10
TEMPTERS	13
EL VAMP YOU SAY YOU LOVE ME?	14
THE LISTENERS	16
DANCE	18
DEMON KEY	20
TEMPLE OF LOVE	23
GANGSTERS AND THIEVES	26
CHESS	35
DRIVER	41
A NOTE FROM GRANDMA	43
LOVE TO BE WORN	44
HONEYMOONED	47
EMBRACED	50
SURPRISE	52
BIRTH	54
IN MY MATRIARCH'S WOMB	56
FLAWLESS FROM SEEDS TO GEMS	58

IT	61
THE EXPELLER PRESS	64
I SAW IT	66
CAT'S EYES	68
ANGEL KEY	70
URBAN NOMAD	72
DEVELOPING	75
WE PRAY	78
TANGERINE SKIES	80
MOSQUITO	82
SUGAR MOUNTAINS	84
MUM THE HUNTER	86
THE COACH	90
MAHARAJA'S PALACE	96
A SOLDIER CALLED "GUY"	100
THE ROADWORKERS	103
THE VILLAGES	106
BEYOND THE THRESHOLD	108
TREAD CAREFULLY	110
SKI CRASH	112
BIKE ADRENALINE MODE	116
WAR	120
SNOWBALL	122

GAMER	126
BEACON	128
THE BARBER SHOP	130
RE - IGNITED	134
VENOM OF CHANGE	135
ACQUISITION	138
ILLUSION'S KEY	141
BORN	144
MAHOGANY CRADLE	145
LOVE DANCE	146
THE PLEDGE	147
BAKERS' SACRAMENT	149
YOU LOVE ME	151
GOLDEN CHALICE	152
SMALL AXE BIG TREE	154
ALIVE	157
EDEN'S CHILDREN	158
ELIXIR'S CHILDREN	160
SLEEP & MEDITATION, THE SILENT ORACLES	162
"GUIDE OF SOULS"	165
HEROES	168
THE ASCENDANCY	170
THE SCULPTOR	174

LETTER TO THE DEPARTED	176
WISDOM COMES QUIETLY	178
AFTERWARDS	180
WE ANGELS	182
THE BATTLE	185
THE GOOD NEWS	188
TO AIDN I CAME	194
A NEW PLANE	198

FOREWORD

Welcome, you have just opened the door to a treasure chest of word music, powerful images and amazing art. Within "Secrets and Keys" are poems that speak of the forces of good, of corruption and the omnipresence of positive energy.

The ebb and flow within life's intricate journey.

By using antonyms of key words Mervin has magically transformed certain poems. Examples can be found in "Demon Key" that has miraculously been reborn into "Temple of Love" There is "Jealousy's Beast" that is translated into "The Pledge" and "Gangsters and Thieves" that re-emerges as "The Good News". This simple principle may be employed in our everyday lives. Negative themes can be re-framed and guided towards kinder pastures whilst gleaning wisdom from the contrast experienced along the way.

There is courage in these poems: everything is laid bare and every subject ripe for exploration and scrutiny. Mervin explores our ideas and our understanding of existence and reality. He stretches our horizons and playfully toys with our perceptions. As such, his poems and art throw challenges at us and leave us with riddles to solve and our own questions to answer. Turn the pages, experience the vision and enjoy the ride.

SPECIAL THANKS

I would like to thank all those who gave their help and encouragement in creating this book of poetry. It has been a long labour of love to gather all the poems and artwork within "Secrets and Keys".

I would like to give a special "thank you" to my mother Eva Kenton who has helped, encouraged and contributed with her art.

Thank you Mother.

Thank you all.

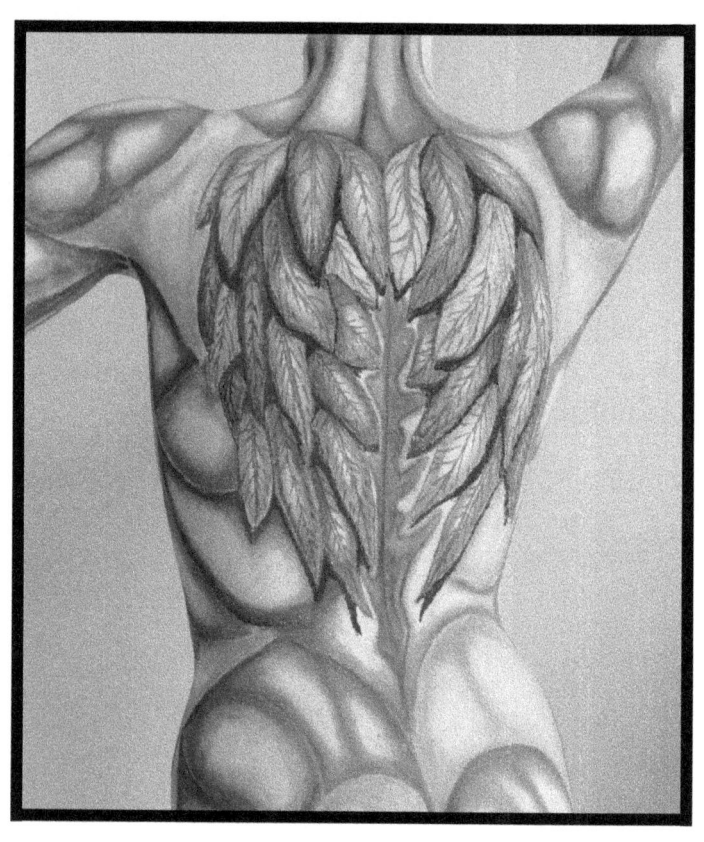

Mervin Telford

AN ODE TO LOVE
1st key

Love is domination tamed,

Cured of its lust for life.

Love is the harried heart

Gone awry with liberation

Made from the pain of

Self denied.

Love is a fresh meadow basking

In the light of its own making.

Is giving only to receive

That which is born by

Blood and joyous tears alike.

Love is ever evolving to the

Prompt of the inner ear

And inner eye.

Love is eternally weighed and

Measured by the unlimited

Scope of the heart.

Love is a suite bestowed

By the grand tailor

And made to fit the light of the

Wearer whose light shines

Brightest in the eyes

Of their beloved.

Love is an internal wish

Heard aloud by creation

And strives only to serve

Especially those who believe

In its offering.

Like the phoenix,

Love rises from ashes

Into flame, again and again.

It impassions Cupid to

Seek his reflection

In the eyes of the enchanted,

Longing for themselves

To be enveloped as one.

Love is pain soothed by

Healing hands.

Is the souls' pounding hooves

Heard then silenced as it

Finds the air with ethereal wings unbound.

Love speaks through

Tips of silken lips that find passion

In that moment of fire,

That flame that bursts forth

From the furnace of life's

Yearning to be absorbed,

A volcanic vortex

Spiralling towards repose.

Love binds us,

Yet it sets us apart,

For its length,

Breadth and wisdom is far beyond us,

Even as it is part of us.

This is love.

JEALOUSY'S BEAST

Anger,
Frustration,
Explosive creation,
Jealousy rises,
Erupting thunderous beast.
It pounds the air,
Comes to feed on elation,
Entwining its victims,
It's the devil's priest.

An aggressor stands screaming,
It's a multiple rage.
A partner stands tear filled,
On a lonely stage.
Thoughts are twisting
And writhing,
It's a sickly display.
A heart verbally assaulted,
Trembling,
Distraught in dismay.

Violent eyes bulge,
Fierce insanity.
Parasitical beast hovers,
Feeding above.
A partner shivers, gently pleading
With beckoning arms outstretched
In love.

As beast spits fire,
The aggressor salivates,
Spraying a poisonous paste.
"ENOUGH!"
Their partner comes to aid in haste.

Beast returns to its caverns,
Its hunger is fed.
The assailant stands depleted
And shakes their head.
Receded jealousy, reformed
They begin to weep.
They are given comfort,
Forgiveness,
And rocked slowly to sleep.

(Please see "The Pledge" page 147)

Eva Kenton

THE STRONG PLACE

How far will we go this time?

Forget,

Into the streams of water,

Forget.

I will not shrink from you.

I will say "yes" and die.

You smile, touch my lips and cry.

"Yes,

I understand, "

See the secrets of your heart revealed.

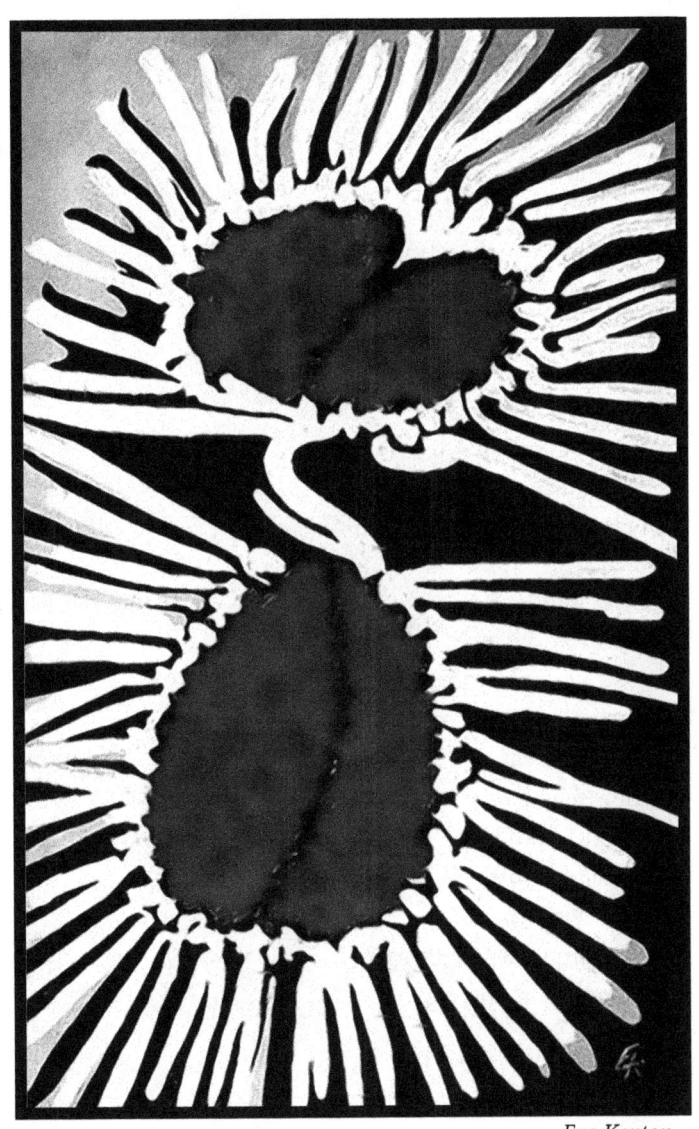

Eva Kenton

TEARS AND FIRE

"Tears and fire",
Do you mean to stay?
Or will you make your peace,
Cast away your weapons
And leave this shore,
Your boat ablaze
Flames dancing from its bow?
Do not be afraid
I will not let you die.
You are my conscience,
My strength or I have none.

"Tears and fire",
You knew me as I was,
Prostrate and forlorn.
You watched the skies with me,
Gave me great faith,
A new name,
A language of hope,
Small steps towards my birthright.
Find joy again,
Live, come away with me?
Aflame again and cry.

"Tears and fire"
Tell them "I am dead,
Into the new realm born."
We are few, but strong as many.

Take out the thorn,
Shed your yoke and ascend with me.
You have made me a believer
And shown me a way and a path.
Now I am married to life,
Bearing precious gifts
And love has made the bond.
Let us go home now,
Live in peace and smile.

We smile.

Mervin Telford

Eva Kenton

TEMPTERS

Primal Promises
Are waiting in their oceans.
People sway
To the spells on their tongues.
A drum beating
To the tempo of desires,
Entrancing the old and the young.

Red, wrapped gifts
Are coiled in their waters.
Foetal and waiting
For the next to come.
Multi-legged and piercing
The hearts of the lonely.
An agenda so delicately spun.

Romeos and Juliets stand bleeding
On illusions, their doorsteps.
Entranced Trojans are
Encaged by their hearts.
Transformed loneliness
Becoming twisted and sculpted,
Proudly they survey their woven art.

EL VAMP
YOU SAY YOU LOVE ME?

They are of a different lineage.
Tortured by a
Hunger that never sleeps.
Internally
They scream for more food.
An insatiable scythe that reaps.
Vacuumed, emptied and meaner,
Their gesticulating victims are
Open mouthed and siphoned.
While the chaos makes
Their Pallet cleaner.

They may say that they love you,
But theirs is not love.

Their mask is vibrantly beautiful.
Hiding the need for a vibrational fix.
The besotted; jostle for position
In a queue that always sticks.
Given neatly dressed leftovers,
A mirage thrown to hungry dogs,
Who chew their tongues like steak?
Because?
El Vamp plays all three characters,
The yellow brick traveller,

The wicked witch
And the god of OZ.

They may say that they love you,
But theirs is not love.

(Please see "You Love Me" page 151)

Eva Kenton

THE LISTENERS

Through chaos moves
A shimmering gown.
Is watched, transfixed
With metered frown.
Through gorging crowd,
To open ear,
Discreetly whispering
Far and near.
Who stood and listened
No longer slept.
They held their heads
Awake and wept.

First breath of words,
Spoke soft to ear,
She shivered,
Turned and ran with fear.
To no avail
She ran and searched.
The remnant words
Afar where perched.
Now old and withered
She realised;
The listeners past
Had held their prize.
Embraced new love,
No longer slept.
Had found new life
And self respect.

Eva Kenton

DANCE

Why?
Why do we cut and paste?
If we have asked for love
And it is given,
Do we try to subtract or add?
Can love be left alone to explore and change?
Or can it be inspired, encouraged and shaped?
Either way,
Do we hold back from love's embrace?
Shy away from a spoken word of love?
A loving touch,
Hug,
Encouragement?

Do we push when we want to pull?
Run when we want to stay?
If so, is it because of fear of failure?
Of rejection,
Of impending hurt?
Or allowing another to see our naked souls
Held to the light and transformed?

Do we fear pleasure's pain?
Searing through our veins,
Pulsating in the depths of our heart and spirit?
Throbbing stomachs,
Aching at the image,
The fleeting thought of the one

We love.
Have grown to love?
Love ourselves to be loved?
How often do we dance with love?

Mervin Telford

DEMON KEY

My parents' world is
Strangely monotone.
Meaningful utterances,
Far and few.
Chaos had entered its bookmarks,
Unsightly and well within view.
Under skin, needles are stinging,
The itch is longing to be fed.
A new thirst is steadily rising.
From "demon key"
A simmering hunger is bred.

The umbilical craving for the elixir,
The gnawing memory of nectar,
Alcohol, smooth and fine,
The raised, reminiscing taste buds,
The "demon key",
Liquid illusions, sublime.

Other children are
In polite conversation,
This child is ignored and confused.
A raised hand
Lowered to impact in anger.
Frustration,
Liquid infused.
The weals from the belt,
Sore and swollen,
To be seen on matriarch and child.

The red of the bloodshot eyeballs,
Of flailing patriarch wild.

Mervin Telford

The Ogre's lair is entered on errand.
Bestial snoring reverberates
Through flatulence filled air.
The Parent sleeps,
Beware,

One eye cyclopic and staring,
One eye closed.
Foetal, drunk,
Indisposed.

A child smells the air
Through a cold edged letterbox.
Nicotine air speaks,
It says, "The parent is home".
The child rearranges its nuances,
Impending pressure,
Emotional vacuum,
Actions unknown.

A child's love replaced with fear
And silent obedience.
The parents' heart grows stagnant and stale.
Their world is ruled by the nightclub,
The pub,
The smoke,
Drugs,
Liquor and ale.
The "demon keys" still has them,
Downward spiral,
In its labyrinth,
See them run wild.
If they could have chosen to be a loving parent,
They may have experienced
The eternal love of a child.

(Please see "Temple of Love" on the next page)

TEMPLE OF LOVE

My parents' world is
Beautifully harmonic.
Meaningful words
Spoken with a sensitive view.
Peace has entered its bookmarks,
Aesthetically pleasing
And well within view.
Comfort and care is radiant.
Our Spirits delicately fed.
Our thirst gently
Quenched by our Guardians.
The angelic prevail overhead.

The need to give love,
Care and affection.
The memory of a helping hand.
Alleviating with food,
Care and shelter.
Feeding the gardens
That a loving God planed.
The reminiscent overture.
Angels shine light all around.
A heavenly requiem surrounds us.
Princes and princesses
Victoriously crowned.

As children we are happy
And playing.
Guardians attentive and kind.
Healing balms,
A hand offered in friendship.
Humbled, we are
Watered and dined.
Spiralling ever skyward.
Majestically soaring
On golden, feathered wings.
The medicinal light
Ever pulsing.
Prayers spoken
For all that life brings.

The angel's domain
Is entered on errand.
Scented and aromatic.
Fragrance filled air.
The family sleeps.
Safely protected.
Tutored in dreams with care.
Sacred eyes focused.
Holy of holies.
Earthly eyes closed,
Foetal,
Gently composed.

A child smells the air
From a soft - edged blanket.
Perfumed breeze speaks,
It says, "Mother is home".
Arms outstretched.
Faces with smiles on.
Hugs and kisses
And on the roam.
Toys and games,
Lessons for fledglings.
Slowly polished
To diamond from stone.

A child's love, priceless,
Thoughtful and contented.
The parents' heart floats.
A ship at full sail.
Their world is ruled by kinship,
Knowledge, wisdom,
Humility and courage in travail.
Love's embrace, it still has them.
Upward spiral,
In its mansions
See them run free.
They chose to be loving parents.
Their legacy always in me.

GANGSTERS AND THIEVES

Sshshh, do you see it?
Something's not right!
Just out of sight.
A black hole full of promises
From falsely elected leeches,
With dark eyes,
Holding hidden lies
Propagating Al- Qaeda
Fear agenda death speeches.
Rehearsed, evaded questions
About missing monies,
Assassinations
And security breaches.
Toppling towers
Give rise to more questions.
While the card dealer hides his hand
And preaches
To hate those who would explode.
A dangerous road.
Who are they?
What do they look like?
They say "Casino,
It's a gamble",
"Anyone of colour"
The bars hidden code.
And guess who's paranoid?
"Uncle Sam"

And it's spreading,
Ask the Guantanamo man.
The people are annoyed.
Mass hypnosis,
Homeland security destroyed.
Global empathy is now redundant,
And the cartoonists are overjoyed.
"Freedom of speech" they say
"Is abundant"
A lie
Means the eye of the bull is red
And on the prophet's head.
Bull's eye.

Eva Kenton

People swaying in the winds,
Like bending weeds.
While the planet is ruled
By gangsters and bled by thieves.

Sshshh, quiet,
Do you hear it?
Something's not right,
Strange,
Just out of range.
My people are dying.
Injected,
Government anti –virus,
Virus.
Scratching poverty,
The children are crying.
Infected,
Saliva drying.
Swollen bellies.
Hunger warns
With swarms.
Egg laying vermin is flying.
God save the West,
And all the diseased obese,
Shop till you drop mentality,
Panic buying,
Liposuction
And a cosmetic feast,
Face surgery
With the cameras spying.

While the sizzling barbeques
Monosodium Glutamate
Half-pound burgers are frying.
Help,
People are needlessly dying.

People,
Swaying in the winds
Like bending weeds.
While gangsters and thieves
Rule the Planet
Yet no one believes.

Shhhshh, quiet.
Do you smell it?
Breathe,
Something's not right!
Burning flames visible,
On screen,
Yet out of sight.
Sectarian violence,
Political wars,
Monitory expansion!
Room for thought and pause?
Coincidence?
Zipped body bags.
From conflicts
Triggered by lies,
And international incidents.
And fake looks of surprise.

G8 gang bangers in suits
Bring divide and rule manifestos,
Agenda Mafioso.
Privatisation = monopolisation
Means polluted planet,
Scientists say probably,
America says so-so.
Government drugs,
From government thugs.
Toxic foods
Mesmerising periodically
On 24 hour screens.
The new oracles,
Blood,
Lust,
Music,
And video games.
Means
Manufactured
Dysfunctional kids in teams
With internal screams.
Mental anaesthesia.
Orwellian prophecy?
Martin Luther's insights
Kept in Big Brother's deep freezer.
Cryogenic human rights
Means state sanctioned terrorism is made easier.

People swaying in the winds
Like bending weeds.
While gangsters and thieves own the planet,
Yet no one believes.

Eva Kenton

Shhshh, do you feel it?
Something's just not right
Micro chips.
Plastic cards.
Exotic flights.
Partying
And sleepless nights,
Tangoed.
Dancing with invisible money.

Luscious billboards that say
"It's a deal"
Holographic Utopia,
Land of milk and honey.
Formula,
Elite tried and tested.
Ritualised
And blood invested.
The reptile's coils are tightened.
Peoples and nations
Financially squeezed and frightened,
Breathless.
The ruling controller's age-old wonder.
Ruthless.
The time-delayed nightmare.
The lightening,
Then the thunder.
Hypnotic adverts,
Dribbling milk,
Suckling cream from the dream Weaver's cow,
"Buy now"
(Misleading comfort)
"Pay later"
While choking in the magnetised debt crater.
Reminders and bills like quicksand
And every bank is a debtor hater
Detonator,
Energy siphon.
The picture has to be bigger.

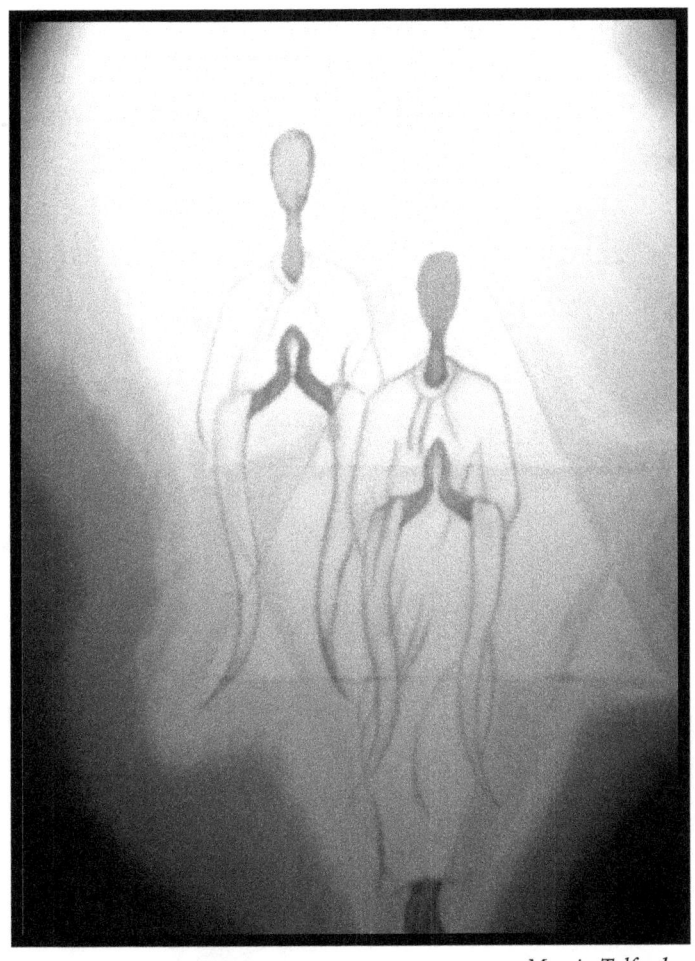

Mervin Telford

The gun is loaded
Wake up and remember
It's our collective finger on the trigger.

And the angel-spirits cry,
"Re-awaken and unite. Stop swaying in the winds like bending weeds. Stop being ruled by gangsters and bled by thieves"

(For antonyms please see "The Good News" page 188)

CHESS

Abandon all hope
Ye of simple mind,
Of peaceful notions,
Gentle and kind.
Hope for more
But leave with less,
For this is life's metaphor,
The riddle called chess.

Prowling Matriarch,
Fear felt but unseen,
Revered above all,
Life begins with the Queen.
Kingdoms rise,
Or Kingdoms fall.
Conquering her enemies
Large or small.
She moves straight and diagonal
Against the marauding hoard.
She holds a regal demeanour
In the defence of her Lord.
With their strategy flawed,
Inner craniums are scratched,
Nigh barren of thought.
Shrewd plans are hatched,
Time compacted and expanded,

No room to think.
Speed chess,
One move?
"Check Mate?"
Sink.

Practically immobile,
A virtual recluse,
The board's director
Irate and obtuse,
Relies on his subjects
His battles to win.
Assigning Mensa strategies,
This brings us to King.
His enemies assail him,
He tries vainly to hide,
One square at a time.
He's the pride of his bride.
The enemy is vanquished,
Outfoxed, on the run.
He basks in the glory
As they fall and succumb.
On the throne sits a lion,
Elevated by pride.
His kingdom rejoices
Lioness by his side.

Religious fervour,
The Diagonal reaper
Wields his scythe.

Blessings are given
To allies who fight.
"God" says the bishop,
"Blesses the battle"
Delight!
He moves with twin
From left and right.
He hides with pawns
Well out of sight.
Coiled,
With breath baited,
Cloaked,
He strikes unanticipated.
First to the cause yet avoiding to die.
The battle worn subjects
Are wondering "Why?"

The "Knight and Horse"
An awkward force.
Frustrating,
Deadly,
With no remorse.
The shape is "L"
As they leap from hell.
Multidirectional,
Jumping as if by spell.
The knight's horse jumps
Up or down,
Left or right,
Two squares then one,

Unequivocal fun.
With havoc
Unrepentant
They seek to depose,
They leap and strike
With deadly blows.
On empty square,
They jump and stare,
Opponents wish they
were not there.
Baffled and in flight,
Opponents are served,
Game defective,
Jangled,
Unnerved.

Impregnable fortress,
Mobile,
Personal guard to the
King,
Called "Rook", "Tower"
or "Castle",
Sits on the extreme of
each wing.
Defence of the throne
Is a means to an end?
Often with castling
The King he'll defend.
Towering turrets,
Stalwart walls that surround,

Wheeling into battlements
To relentlessly pound.
Moving straight and narrow
So long as it's free.
A thunderous force
By King's decree,
His presence enough
To make enemies flee.

The opposing monarch
He seeks to dethrone.
The flanks of the battlefield
He makes his own.
To his patrons he is priceless,
Next in line to the Queen,
Near the end of the battle
He is usually seen.

The first shall be last
And the last shall be first;
The pawn was born to battle
With unquenchable thirst.
First on the battlefield
As the strategy's revealed,
First to fall
To make enemies stall.
His initial move?
One square or two he may go,
One square thereafter,
One square diagonally

To vanquish his foe.
Last to stand to protect the King,
Death before dishonour,
For dying bereft of courage is sin,
To reach the board's end,
Never again to be seen.
Changed to all bar the King.
Exchanged for a Queen
"Check mate"
Execution unseen.

Mervin Telford

DRIVER

Love is driven,
Made barren at home,
By negligent ears,
Hearing only a downward tone.
Driven by bitter hearts.
By minds that send hurt.
Misguided thoughts,
Oblivious to trust, but not to dirt.

Warmth is inverted
My summer is cold.
Slowly depleted
On solitudes threshold.
The controller's shadow,
Invisible but felt.
My hope is besieged
Where love once dwelt.

My heart bleeds tears
Where cherubs once danced.
My labour is ignored,
Distant listeners entranced.
Jeopardy approaches,
Deployed by the negative tongue.
Humility surrounds me
My destiny is still spun.

Reborn strength,
Risen from the forger's fire.

Volcanic vortex
Rising higher and higher.
The sleeper is awakened.
The lie is cut short.
This hologram's illusion
Can no longer be bought.

(For antonyms please see "Embraced" page 50)

Mervin Telford

A NOTE FROM GRANDMA

Dear Mervy,
Sometimes you will be gifted
A challenging task.
Its magnitude so new
You're wondering what to do,
Visualise yourself get through it and
See it to its end. Now, theoretically,
It has already been done.
So you go ahead and do it for real.
Because you know it can work,
Even if others say "it might not".
It doesn't matter
You've already begun.
Because you know it can work you
Try different ways until it's done.
Ask for assistance if you need to
Because some things need help
Or turn out differently.
But it doesn't matter
Because you've practiced
And learned to visualise
Things go right. So more things will do,
You believe and you've seen them.
So theoretically you've been there before.
So now things will be better,
You know they can be
And so they are. This makes you happy,
Which makes you smile,
Because you can.

To Mervy from your Gran X

LOVE TO BE WORN

Love
Suits you
You should wear it more often.
Out in the open
As a token
Of good
Will

It
Is
A
Joy
To see
Smiles because
Love really suits you.
You should wear it more often.
Out in the open,
As a token
Of good
Will
It
Is
A
Joy
To see
Happiness as
Love really suits you
You should wear it more often.
Out in the open
As a token
Of good
Will
It
Is
A
Joy
To see
Laughter as

Love really suits you
You should wear it more often.
Out in the open
As a token
Of good
Will
It
Is
A
Joy
To feel
Loved as
Love really suits you
You should wear it more often.

Love   Love
I love you I love you
I love you I love you
I love you I love
You love I
I love
I

HONEYMOONED

What if,
We saw ourselves shining,
Fresh and shimmering,
Feeling the rising
Heat of the pheromone.
Hunger aroused to
Fine dining,
Melting chocolate
On caramel,
Swollen strawberry yearning.
What if
We felt merging lights,
Fiery innards burning,
Whites of eyes
Turned sky high,
Eternally embraced,
Out of control,
And no longer shy.
Mesmerised with wings,
Entwined and spinning,
Global spirits turning?
What if we were
Falling through the air,
Lost in ourselves
Wet, unrestrained
Lovers singing.
Gently shivering
A thousand times a minute,

Glowing and shaking,
Gulping breaths,
Lightning exploding.
Held still and sunken
In sweet dripping sweat,
Silently embracing
Togetherness and understanding.

Perhaps today
We would be voyeurs
Glimpsing passions cocktail
Of magnetised erotica.
Mental flashbacks
And rewinds,
Eager minds wanting more,
Waiting to press the
Memory's stop button
And explore.
Perhaps we would have
Hidden reactions?
Wild then tamed, simmering,
Waiting for a re-run,
Last night's pleasures,
Again and again.
What if right now
We enjoy the glance,
The word,
The pretence of chance,
The slightest touch,
The stayed embrace,
Shared special moments,

The smile on the face,
Because something good
Had been added
Through providence,
Patience and grace,
Not to be taken away,
We pray.
Wouldn't that beautiful?

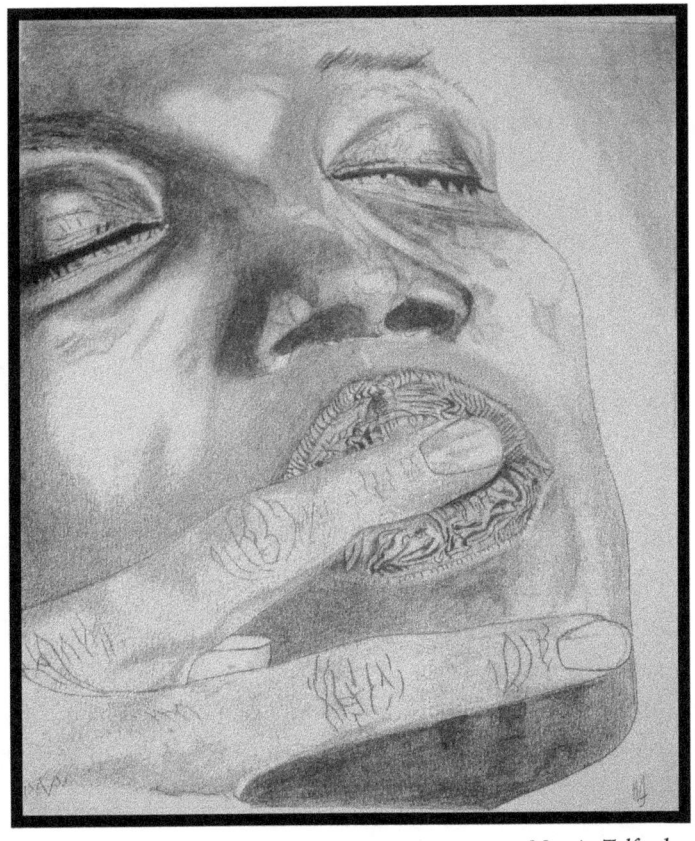

Mervin Telford

EMBRACED

Warmth that's inviting
Our summer is gold,
Love is released
From friendship's threshold.
A benevolent presence
Invisible but felt.
Our faith has flourished
Where empathy is spelt.

Comfort is magnified
Made bountiful at home,
By diligent ears,
Hearing a beautiful tone.
Attracted by a sweetened heart,
By a mind that sent love.
Guided thoughts,
Attentive to trust,
Within a clean head start.

Our hearts glow, shining,
Where Cherubs now dance.
Our future is exciting,
Loves' listeners entranced.
Sanctity approaches,
Deployed by the positive tongue.
Blessed to be grateful.
Our destiny is spun.

Strength Reborn,
Risen from the forgers' fire.
Volcanic vortex'
Swirling axis,
Rising higher and higher.
As lovers we have awakened,
Truth's sacred escorts.
Joyous sweet visions,
Embraced,
Beautiful thoughts.

SURPRISE

Her voice touches me now

And she sings, sings a song with me,

Then basks in sweet silence,

Her heightened senses

Inquisitive, bold and free.

Heart, mind and spirit

Surprise,

They always surprise.

My song echoes

Into the soul of her,

Into the heart of her,

Into the reflection in her eyes

And we rise,

Together we rise.

Eva Kenton

BIRTH

With devotions established
The covenant is signed.
Two destinies become one,
And peace soothes over
Spirit, body, mind.

Fuelled by love and deep respect,
Emotions are afire,
The furnace is set.
Crimson moon
Casts its shadow to show,
Two entwined bodies
On the land below.

Embryo feeds,
Sleeps,
Delicate ball.
For life pumps blood
In womb so small.
Radiant mother,
She eats with care,
Baby thrives,
Food enough to share.

Worried Father,
Mother is helped.
She walks so much slower,
The weight is felt.
Mother guides father's hands,
He feels,
Baby kicks with tiny heels.

Mother shows large,
Babe has grown.
Birth day is here,
She begins to groan.
Excited father,
Alarms are raised.
Sweating,
Panic subdued,
Face crazed.

Racing car,
Speeding wheelchair,
Bed.
Strong contractions,
He holds her head.
Doctors,
Nurses manoeuvre around.
Father is trembling,
Numb,
Baby has come.
Nurse takes baby
Smacks bum.

Mother exhausted,
Babe in embrace.
Smiling Father.
Exuberant face.
All are soon home.
Babe wrapped warm.
Thanking the creator,
Their child is born.

IN MY MATRIARCH'S WOMB

The tapestry's needle is
Threaded with care,
In answer to life's longing
And her indefinite prayer.
Distant voices,
Audible bubbling,
Raw fluids that flow,
I am the arrow
That waits to be sent by the bow.

Liquid confinement,
Struggling,
Born, yet unborn,
Claustrophobic,
I move my tiny form.
Nurturing care,
Soothing waves of concern from above,
How close the voice
That speaks of sweet solace and love.

Echoes travel my chamber
As I move gently around,
Sharp noises,
Mechanical whining,
Musical melodies sound.
Yet when all is silent,
Two audible harmonies pulsate as one,
They reassure me,
My tapestries course must be run.

Pandemonium,
Panic,
Heart pulsating,
Frantic with dread,
As intense forces bend bones,
Sending pains through my head.
Intensifying tightness,
Squeezing from head to toe,
Then released into brightness,
I'm sent forth by the bow.

Choking fluids,
Applied suction,
They said "Breathe": I obeyed!
Assaulted,
Washed,
Dried,
Measured and weighed.
Alien noises surround me,
Nebulous forms stand and stare.
My matriarch receives me
And feeds me with care.

FLAWLESS
FROM SEEDS TO GEMS

We are flawed,
Imperfect,
Yet perfect in our imperfection.
A babe is born.
If it is deemed physically normal
And pleasing to the eye,
Its parents proclaim, "It is perfect"
Yet it cannot talk,
It cannot walk,
It cannot feed
Or defend itself.
Where, deep in the diamond mine
Was a precious jewel
Ever found shining,
Perfectly cut and flawless?
Nowhere!
It is found raw and dull,
Yet full of potential.

What if, in your dream
A precious stone had a voice
And found itself being squeezed,
Cut and polished whilst in the grip
Of a benevolent jeweller's vice.

Would you tell it to wail and
Shout "no more pain"?
Would you tell it to struggle free
And run screaming "let me stay
Unfinished and undefined,
Please no more pain"?
Or would you tell it to stay
And see out its temporal condition.
Doing its best,
Enduring without question
And having faith and trusting
The sharp and rasping edges of the jeweller's tools?
Knowing that it was on the path
To its full potential and glory ?
What would you tell it to do ?

Many see those with growing pains
And perceive only imperfection.
They point saying "imperfect fool,
Why doest thou suffer so?
I am better and suffer not, therefore
I am superior, do as I say".
A wise man knows
"The fool and the master
 Are one and the same",
Except that a true master
Sees the fool in himself,
But the foolish see only themselves.

A wise man understands
That he knows little,
Yet silently he perceives much.
Continually he strives to glean
Knowledge and wisdom
From all experiences.
He sees potential, growth
And beauty in all beings.

Mervin Telford

IT

"It" escapes us and evades us,
"It" ages and delays,
"It" sketches fond old memories
As we remember
Our struggling days.

"It" draws us to the future,
Bringing many to their knees,
Is upon us within seconds,
Despite the resistant pleas.

"It" brings cruelty
And leaves reason,
But the anguish still remains,
As it's "It" that will deplete us
Despite our resistant strains.

For many try to oppose "It's" will
Seeking chemicals and cures,
They cling to youth and beauty,
Despite their hidden flaws.

Some lower their resistance
When they slowly realise
That it rules them with persistence
For "It" sleeps with open eyes.

"It" watches those who oppose it,
Those who disobey its laws
With their operations,
Cures and potions,
They look for loud applause.

But some know their episode
Will soon be over, when
They see grey hair, wrinkled skin
Then something stirs inside them,
Something deep within.

Some look below the surface
For something clean and pure,
Some look for what will guide them
To a destiny secure.

A man lays looking skyward,
Having found his peace
In love and faith.
He feels relaxed and tranquil,

Radiant smile comes to his face.

The clocks hand nears the hour,
His breath grows weak and frail,
His ship soon leaves the harbour
And homeward it will sail.

His family stand there lonely.
His daughter sits and cries,
His eyes they close so slowly.
The clock begins to chime.

"IT" IS TIME.

Mervin Telford

THE EXPELLER PRESS

Unexpectedly
Freedom woke me,
Whispering in my ear,
"Every day is Christmas day
It's not just once a year."
"I like surprises" I smiled and thought,
"Under the green tree today,
What surprises await me?
What delightful gifts have been bought?"

Again freedom whispered in my ear,
"Gifts don't all come sweetly wrapped.
Some come wrapped in toil and fear,
And with some you'll shed a tear.
Some bring bravery out of danger,
Will take you to the brink,
Build characters, make heroes,
Making many swim or sink.
Be wise and thankful in advance
For these valuable, deceptive woes,
Giving precious oil
From the expeller press,
Helping humanity towards repose".

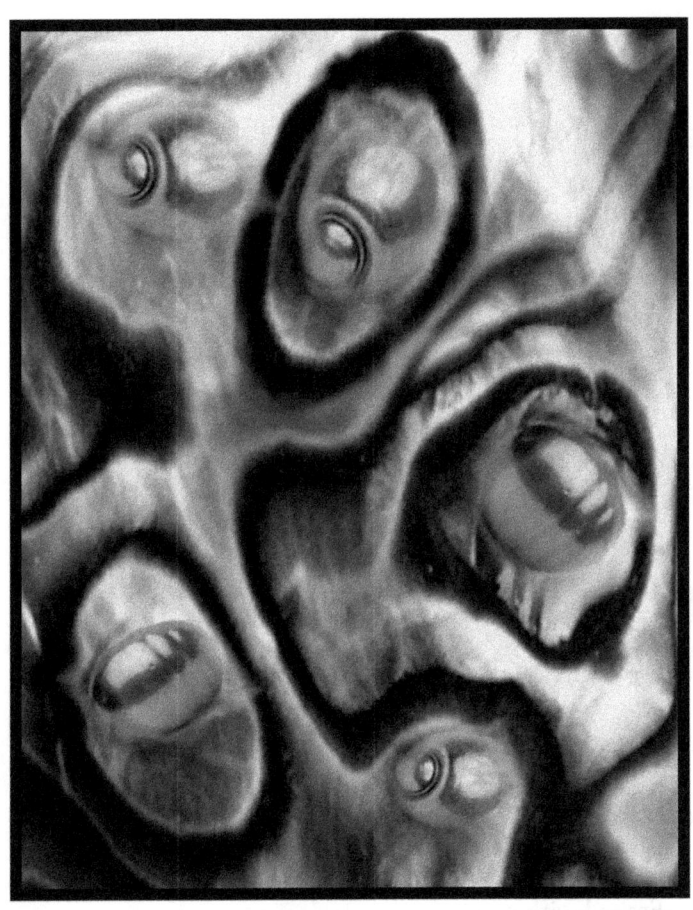

Mervin Telford

I SAW IT

I yearned,
Longing
To touch
With tongue.
Wet lip of mine,
Exploring,
The smooth and folds
Of your passionate mouth.

Then, I saw it?

My longing
For yours only.
Silken and beckoning.
To sign
My name.
Sweet centre of speech,
Etched with care.
Extended initials of closeness.

Then, I saw it?

Your nose on his.
Fury lips touching,
Semi frenching,
Nuzzling the petals
Once mine alone, I thought?
His rigid body,
Extended at your touch
And when you momentarily
Put him to rest.

Then, I saw it?

He turned inwards
And licked his backside.
I stop short of sharing
Your lips with a cat's bottom.
Graceful though he may be.
Your lips have been bittered,
Soured at his touch.
He has a clean backside perhaps!
But at what expense?

No kisses for you my dear.

I bid you farewell forever,
Because I saw it.

CAT'S EYES

The flap opens silently against my head,
As I leave behind the digs where I get kissed and eat the crap stuff.
I arch and stretch limbering up before I enter the territories.
This patch is mine.
I hunt
And I suffer no trespassers.

Dark clouds drift silently overhead,
Suffocating the moonlight.
I effortlessly probe the black suede of night.
Momentarily suspended are other eyes.
Luminous,
Fixed, silent and waiting,
For round two, three and so on.

Clumps of fur stuck in the Hawthorn tree
Trigger memories of whiplash, flashing claws,
Glistening fangs and spinal screams at midnight.
They and I still bear the scars.

With a black velvet coat,
My camouflage is black,
On this black starless night.
I hunt
And I suffer no trespassers.

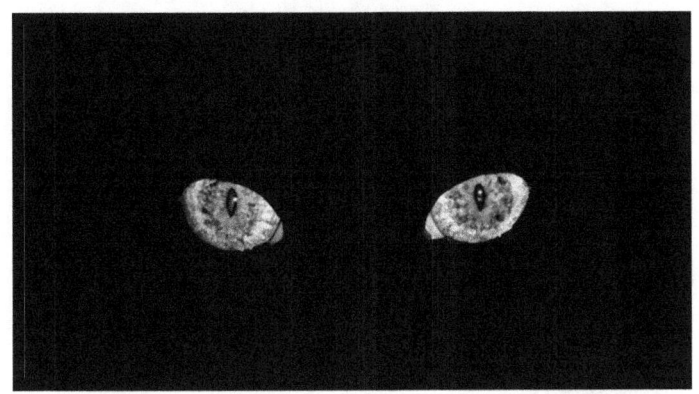

Mervin Telford

ANGEL KEY

I am alarmed.
Made vulnerable.
Disarmed.
A sudden mute.
Covered in flames,
That tri-radiate
From your central sun
That reigns.
Stilled are foolish concerns of self.
For I have come upon new wealth.
My vanity is made void.
By your resonance,
The "ID" is destroyed.
I am now a king again,
By your Angel Key
Made sane.

Ego is shaken
From its throne,
And assigned as servant,
I have grown.
Unshackled from uncouth,
I am mesmerised
And entranced by truth.
The Original "I am"
Is translated through your eyes.
Innocent transistor crystals.
Mirrors of surprise.
In your presence

The riotous are made tranquil,
And beasts of prey made tame.
Firestorms diverted,
Floods and hurricanes,
Made lame.
Conflict turned to calm,
By your grace and loving charm.
Ancient energies reside
Respectfully by your side.
Covered in a cloak of light,
Warm fire burning bright.
In you I see
The Angel Key.
For as you are true to thee,
I am now true to me.
Set free.

Eva Kenton

URBAN NOMAD

Life's hammer chisels relentless still,
As worn body struggles
Along this endless hill.
Winter breeze bites into flesh exposed,
Face, hands and feet are freezing,
Despite his warm ragged clothes.

Hair hangs wild from head and jaw,
As faded memories recall comforts,
Memories of a warm home
And the love that shines no more.
Memories of youth,
When rash decisions later made laughter
And loud exciting talk.
When dares where done for fun
And in friendship he would walk.

But now he passes the restaurants,
His nostrils devour their smells,
He stares through inviting windows,
As exotic foods cast irresistible spells,
With their compassion assaulted,
The customers turn and glare,
They look out at him disgusted,
They wish he was not there.
Now his stomach shows its displeasure
With nagging hunger pains,
He probes and searches the rubbish bins
For edible remains.

Eva Kenton

His aching legs are cold and shaky,
Nearly totally fatigued.
Sleep's need is now emerging
And shows it must be freed.
Soothing warmth is a luxury,
But dry shelter is soon found,
He takes his makeshift materials
And wraps them all around.
The cold begins to penetrate
His fragile warm enclose,
He slowly divorces his connections
From his numb and freezing toes.

In dreams he senses wonderful colours
And greets old friends in partial flight,
Ahead is a luminous tunnel,
He is drawn near by its alluring light.
He feels magically ecstatic,
He feels he's finally free,
The permeating beauty
Of this visual melody.
In the morning they find him,
Mucus hanging on frozen face,
He looks from above shining,
Departed into heavenly grace.

(Please see "Bakers' Sacrament" page 149)

DEVELOPING

I travelled.
Today I saw things
That will never allow me to
Complain about hardship again.

I saw paid washer men
Stand knee deep
In grime laden water,
Systematically cleansing
Clients soiled laundry.
Stinking foul water,
Water wrinkled hands,
Slapping dirty soaked sheets
On wet stone slabs,
Over and over.
Heat filled labour,
Hour after hour,
Day after day,
Treading ,
Scrubbing,
Rinsing,
Rubbing.

I travelled.
Today I saw things
That will never allow me to
Complain about hardship again.

I saw children
Robbed of their childhood by poverty.
A begging hand,
Outstretched in hope,
A tug at the sleeve,
Relentless,
Unceasing,
Asking,
Tear filled pleading,
Following,
Waiting.
A ragged blind man walks the street,
Slowly tapping his blind stick.
The whites of his eyes roll skyward,
As if in silent prayer,
The name of his god is continually
Chanted by his shrill voice,
A voice made obscure by the crowd,
By their familiarity with his plight.

I travelled.
Today I saw things
That will never allow me
To complain of hardship again.

A dog walks awkwardly
Weaving through the crowd.
I look again closely,
I see surreal twisted vertebrae,
Gnarl jointed,

Protruding bones:
This is no dog,
It is a man,
Severely deformed.
He walks on all fours,
Begging as he does so.
He is passed overhead,
Ignored by the crowds,
Long ago made numb,
Desensitized by the limbless,
The blind,
Diseased,
Deformed,
Children of poverty,
Who search for a charitable hand,
Their emblem of survival.

I travelled.
Today I saw things
That will never allow me
To complain of hardship again.

(Please see "To Aidn I Came" page 194)

WE PRAY

We pray.

In the silence of our hearts,

Or in the forefront of our minds,

Or through speech

We wish for love and this and that.

Intently the universe listens,

And in the fullness of time

It delivers and we receive

Our allotted portion.

Why then do we ask for more of a gift?

Why do we say, "this is not as it should be"?

Remember then our past

Thoughts, words and actions.

Has not the universe been gracious and true

In its listening and its offering?

So be conscious for what it is that you wish for

And careful in which manner you wish.

Eva Kenton

TANGERINE SKIES

Hippopotamus heads
Are floating,
Dark islands.
A large silhouette stands
With siphoning trunk.
The mammoths descendent is swaying
While the Zambezi's waters are gently drunk.

Sunlit skies,
Strawberry streaks,
Reds merge into oranges.
Tangerine clouds
Pierced with horizontal yellow hues.
Our dancing retinol receptors are dining
On a feast of spectacular dusk views.

On the horizon
The disc of fire is slowly sinking.
Glowing,
Orange-yellow,
Giant ball of the sun.
Sharp palms cast lazy long shadows
As insects play symphonies,
Nocturnal melodies have begun.

Fragrance inhaled,
Rich and moist,
Tropical sunset.
Visually breathed in with easy eyes.
The boats hull slides
By croaking frogs
Through trickling waters.
Our breeze-caressed faces
Are dazzled by tangerine skies.

Mervin Telford

MOSQUITO

Heated scent carries fragrances,
Delicious,
Addictive,
Glutinous pheromone soup.
Sweet and sour odours,
Spicy and heady.
Nectarious red gloop.
Honeyed haemoglobin,
Alluringly wafting
In the tropic steam of night.
Humid, liquid promises,
Seductively enticing and in flight.
Hungry wings busily flicker,
Carrying with charismatic ease,
They that sing by buzzing
And sting and feed as they please.

In the magnetising aroma,
A symphonic buzzzzz haunts the air.
Ambrosial claret oozes
Into they that drink without care.
The restaurants' diners are gorging
As skin wrapped food snoozes fair,
Host to a self-service gourmet.
When awake the donor goes spare.
To scratch at the scraps, nails are tearing,
And victims curse the air,
As they that sing with buzzing
Elsewhere sting and feed without care.

Mervin Telford

SUGAR MOUNTAINS

Today heaven sent sugar,

Trickling powder from the stars,

Glistening,

White cotton flakes falling.

Pines cones covered

Like white cigars.

The sugar is staying,

Obeying,

Lying thick,

Sweet,

Yet unsweet.

We with elongated footwear

Zigzag and glide with hard bound feet.

The senses are spiralling and reeling.

Rear skis spraying powder,

White dust at high speed.

We fly unabated on Sugar Mountains,

Skis jumping.

Adrenals pumping.

Souls freed.

Eva Kenton

MUM THE HUNTER

New prey is needed,
New destinations found,
Hunting grounds for this hunter,
Child of a hunter,
Trapper of trappers,
Who searches worldwide.
A quest for the perfect kill,
The thrill,
The exhilaration,
The rush,
Holding in hand
Power to ensnare the moment.
The more remote,
The more tribal,
The more unseen,
The more unusual the better.
Then "SNAP" goes the shutter.

Truck,
Jeep,
Horse,
Donkey,
Camel riding,
Desert trekking,
Climbing.
Sometimes for days,
Scrambling over sun tarnished rock,

Ravenous lens,
Twitching trigger finger,
Constantly on vigil.
Then the prize:
The villager,
Historic ruin,
Unusual flora,
The breathtaking landscape.
Then "SNAP" goes the shutter.

Wide-eyed Germanic,
Wild Jaeger,
Tracking with wide angle,
Macro,
Zoom.
Walking, running,
Crawling,
Stalking.
Trying to focus
On bended knee,

Sideways,
Up a tree,
Could be a fanatic.
Balancing
Precariously
On a glacier.
Then "SNAP" goes the shutter.

Persistent,
Yogurt drinking,
Bug resistant,
Bargaining for the perfect portrait,
Enticing for the perfect smile,
Cursing the clouds,
An unending quest.
Hurriedly changing memory cards,
Lenses,
Cameras.
Collecting visual experiences,
Vivid images,
After dinner conversation pieces.
Going to were no man has been before,
Picture hungry Cyclops,
Pointed,
Aimed at the ready,.
Held steadily,
Held breath.
Then "SNAP" goes the shutter.

Once home the kill is exhumed,
Resurrected,
Precious
Two-dimensional trophies,
Poured over,
Examined for hours,
Sleepless nights,
And anxious days,

The treasure,
Gathered,
Sorted,
Colour rearranged,
Enlarged,
Printed,
Cropped,
Snipped and glued,
Put to disk and viewed.
All because "SNAP" went the shutter.

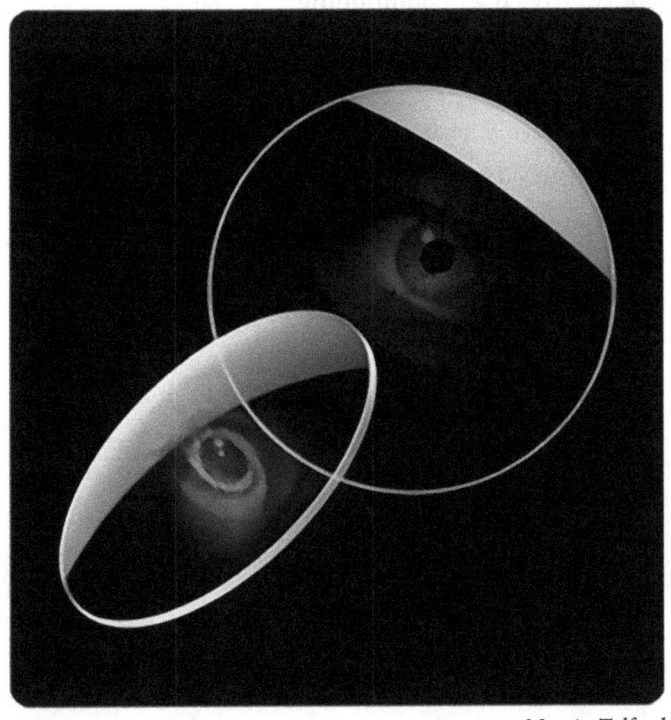

Mervin Telford

THE COACH

With courtesy,
The coach,
Indian luxury,
For us.
Volunteers on wheels,
Paying clientele,
No expense spared,
Slide open windows
For controlled air conditioning.
Rattled,
Gentle at first,
Then gradually harder,
Till we can't think straight any more.
Heated,
Till our pores,
Laden with sweat,
Swell,
Crack and burst,
Oozing,
Trickling,
Dripping from eyebrows
Into well concealed grimacing faces,
With no expense spared.

But we stay in control
Because we're British, you know.

We drive through a town,
Dirt,
Fume rich,
Fragrant thick air
Accosts our nostrils.
Dust ricochets off eyeballs,
I blink repeatedly.
We close the windows to escape,
Only to be confined,
Mentally struggling with the heat.
Sweat forms on foreheads,
Beading,
Regrouping,
Ready for the attack,
To descend,
To conquer
The hope filled faces,
Languishing beneath.

But we remain quiet and resolved
Because we're British, you know.

We drive clear of the town,
Eagerly,
Windows open for reprieve.
Flared nostrils
Hungrily inhale new air,
But are greeted by
Simmering,
Pungent,
Incense of fertiliser,
Mammalian waste.
Heat vaporized,
Soil nutrient,
Launching consistent assaults
One after the other
On bewildered, confused,
Delicate western nose buds.

But our countenance remains calm
Because we're British, you know.

The coach is shaking us,
Rocking us from side to side.
Vertically,
Horizontally,
Diagonally,
Then suddenly, level road.
Relative calm,
Embracing,

Inward sighs of relief,
But only for a moment.
We have been lulled
Self deceptively
For the rattling soon returns,
Gradually,
Intensifying,
To a seeming crescendo.
Something will fall apart very soon,
And it's likely to be us, the occupants.

But we remain polite and expectant
Because we're British, you know.

We feel the force,
Tremors,
Fierce vibration,
Stronger,
Tougher, harder,
Longer.
Stomach churning hard vibrations,
Working to hold onto breakfast vibrations,
Character building vibrations.

But here we sit nonchalant
Because we're British, you know.

I visualise contorted faces.
If I did give in,
Let the floodgates open,
Gushing vomit,
Slippery floor,
Odour filled silence of disbelief,
Even disgust.
This dreadful image assists me
In restraining the mutinous liquid,
Gurgling,
Straining to come forth
To really spoil my day.
I wonder if I'm the only one?
I search the hollow faces
Of my fellow travellers.
I see buttock clenching,
Flatulent faces of despair,
Sunken eyed, pallid faces,
Resisting emotion faces.

And our lips remain stiff
Because we're British, you know.

Mervin Telford

MAHARAJA'S PALACE

The coach swung around
The base of the hill.
There it was,
Splendid, glorious !
From a bygone age,
The Maharaja's palace.
Perched on the hilltop,
Emanating magnificence
From balconies,
Turrets and
doorways.
Hallways
whispered
historically
Of the rich and the
regal,
Who's imagined
shadows
Are cast on its floors.
Impressive ?
Through the tall arches
Into the main hall,
Impressive changed to incredible.

Antique wooden panels
Clung halfway
To the high walls.
Rugs and animal skins

Clothed the floors.
On the walls
Hung ghost faces,
Rhino,
Deer,
Leopard,
Antelope,
Bear,
Tiger,
Impala,
It goes on and on.
Stuffed,
Rewards of the archaic playing fields.
The good old boys.
Inspired by the colonialist
Shouts of "Tally ho".
Images of death surround,
Death is what awaits.
For it is this house that is now dying.

Maharaja,
How can death surround you so ?
How can a house flourish so ?
You rekindle your history fondly
But lack foundation for the present,
To start anew for the future.
Antiquity surrounds you,
Unwittingly you have built a crypt,
A house for murdered nature.
Your trophies' souls

Patiently await their release,
For your house is dying.
Deemed structurally defective,
Your walls are crumbling,
Your land is drying
Through drought and neglect.
Yet you build a swimming pool.
How,
Maharaja,
Will your guests swim in dust?

The tigers,
Stuffed and nailed to your walls,
Though long dead,
Their eyes have life
More than your own.
For I see you smile,
But not from your soul.
I hear you talk,
But not from your heart.
You show us your palace,
With dignity ? Yes.
With fond memories? Yes.
But there is sadness,
I see it in your eyes.
How long,
Maharaja
Till the earth reclaims its own ?
How long

Till your treasured trophies
Are received by the soil
That they where stolen from ?
How long
Till you are blind no more ?
How long
Maharaja,
How long ?

A SOLDIER CALLED "GUY"

"I'm standing here
Staring at black, dark gold,
A fuse into a starless abyss,
Playing a soldiers game
Called "what If?"
If I hadn't seen and heard
Shrill, pained cries
In live red themed paintings,
Martyrdoms BOOOOooooommm
At check point Charley,
Deafening, white flash.
Shattered flesh, red snowflakes rise,
Glide, pause, continue and sail to ground".

"What if
If I hadn't seen and heard,
Body parts slapping the road,
Thudding into dirt,
Strewn pieces of pink that wouldn't fit,
Didn't pop back into the puzzle again
Because the picture was all wrong?
We tried, they failed,
Failed all of us".

"What if
If I hadn't seen and heard
That we'd been ambushed
By our own assassins.

Mervin Telford

Red blades in prim suits
With right arm raised,
Thumb pointing downwards?
Aimed at our backs,
From democracies safe houses.
Friendly fire? Negative creeds
In the arenas for the damned?"

"What if,
If I hadn't seen and heard these things?
Then I wouldn't be standing here
Playing a soldiers game
Called "what if"
Staring at black, dark gold,
A fuse into a starless abyss,
With a detonator in my hand,
Because NO ONE
Is stopping 'Guy Fawkes today".

THE ROADWORKERS

Eva Kenton

New roads need building
A man's work?
No,
Not here.

Lines of women,
Sometimes barefoot,
Move to and fro.
Clouds of grey smoke
Twist and curl in the air.
Rising from bubbling,
Black, liquid tar.
Simmering in heat filled pots,
Glowing roadside furnaces.

A man's work?
No,
Not here.

Perpendicular piles.
Gravel.
Sand.
Slabs of broken old road
Wait to be physically shifted.
Load by load.
Bowl by bowl.
Hoisted onto hardened heads.
These streamline labourers.
Caressed by flowing,
Dust laden,
Colour filled Sari's.

A man's work?
No,
Not here.

Smooth moving,
Sinewy structures.
With heavy vessels
Attached overhead.
Filling, carrying, and emptying.
Bowls filled to the brim.
Balanced on compact vertebrae.
Held steady.
Held strong,
Effortlessly it seems.
A surreal vision,
Moving with grace.
Lithe harmony in motion.
Strong.
Dignified,
Women.

A man's work?
No,
Certainly not here.

THE VILLAGES

I see beautiful faces,
Graceful figures
Gliding in colour rich garments,
Adorned with heavy, engraved silver,
Yet poverty surrounds.

I see craftworks,
Painstakingly created,
Ornately decorated,
Then sold for a pittance
To visiting tourists.
Tourists collecting triggers
For memories of images.
Picture hungry,
Glass eyes
Pointed at the ready.

I see a young child
Oblivious to the swarms
Attached to
The mucus on her face.
Flies crawl in
And out of her ears,
Nose and mouth.
I shudder and wonder
Why the attending old
Woman sits by motionless?
Then I'm told
"She is blind"!

Mervin Telford

BEYOND THE THRESHOLD

Fire, Wind, Water, Earth.

Spirit Father, Mother,

Love and spread your arms.

Guide and strengthen us

To live beyond the threshold

And embrace your natural balms.

Mervin Telford

TREAD CAREFULLY

Lost dreams are like pearls,

Stolen, reclaimed and cast ashore,

Thrown by an infinite sea.

If you walk by the water's edge

Tread carefully

For you may tread on lost dreams.

If you see them naked,

Glistening in the midday sun,

Call out with your thoughts;

We will come to help gather

And nurture them once more.

If you walk by the water's edge

Tread carefully,

For you may tread on lost dreams.

Eva Kenton

SKI CRASH

CRASH,
She didn't see the hole
Beneath the hump.
The humbling hollow
Below the rising bump.
The pit,
Viper,
Waiting to grab hold,
Flick
And jack knife.
To catapult and unfold.
A painful story.
To be told
Re-told, cold and gory.

CRASH,
She didn't see the ski sniper.
Too late.
She was suddenly air born.
A hand me a diaper,
Hyper,
Unwilling sky diver.
Mini
Ski jumper.
Stretched and coronary.
A momentary still life.
Shot from bindings,
Forward spun.
Mentally video recorded
To be re-wound and re-run.

CRASH,
She didn't see the ridge
That led to the slope
Two sides gaping without hope.
But she heard the
"BANG"
That stopped her rudder.
That cranked her neck.
The shipwreck
That made her shudder
And enter the
    Altered
      Reality
        SINKING
      Feeling
    With *ICE* canines
  And SNOW fangs
Under the skin
On the face and neck
Stinging.
A thousand pins
On the inside wanting out.
Scraped red and shaking.
N e c k
S t r e t c h e d
With ears ringing
And a melody of
"Ouches"
Heard singing.

CRASH,
She saw flashes in the sky.
Multicoloured fireflies
Floating in her eyes.
She saw providence
And its gentle pointing hand.
And her ego unable to expand.
She saw fate
That led to tempered seeing.
And soft turns
Down arduous slopes.
That made for graceful skiing
And prolonged well being.
A lesson held in store.

She continued to stumble
But crashed
No more.

Eva Kenton

BIKE ADRENALINE MODE

Sculpture in motion,
Blistering speed,
Shimmering vision,
On a heat-burned road.
Elements exploded!
The rider's body
Forward arched,
Perched in adrenalin mode.
Sleek graphics,
Rear Michelin,
Sticky,
Fat and good.
Wrist twisted,
Throttled with love and devotion,
As any true biker would.

In the engine is an audible fire.
Fresh fuel cools loins for
More fun,
Cars attacking,
A brow raised in anguish,
Death is howling
As he hits a ton.
Anxious nerves,
Wet metal covers,
Road lines like serpents
Lay waiting.
Cracks, holes, humps

Are unrepaired,
Unrepentant and baiting.
But even if he's snapped
Or broken.
If he's catapulted,
Twisted or takes a burn,
Lacerated leathers,
The deep red stain on the tarmac,
Yet he knows he will return.

The ambush,
The yellow box,
A hidden camera.
Awaiting Hayabusa's
Echoing screams.
The itchy trigger finger.
Five O concealed in their teams.
Wet snouts, pigs ears on
The road check.
Old Bill's schemes craftily spun.
Blurred cars, amber lights,
The narrow gap,
The reapers shadow.
SNAP,
The menace of the white flashing gun.

Behold the true enemy
That stalks the rider.
His brain is seared by its will.
His heart has become its

Foundation.
Once smitten
He'll never be still.
Tweaked engine,
Dazzling chrome,
Flawless paintwork.
The need to be braver,
The unattainable feat.
Hammering valves
The growl of the V-twin engine,
Volcanic furnace under the seat.
The quest to be noticed,
A thousand shivers
Alive and smiling
Electricity surging within
To be first,
To be faster.
To be fastest.
The unquenchable thirst to win.

Mervin Telford

WAR

Sweet mothers,
Sisters tear their hair.
Widows lament and wail.
Lay sobbing
Into the night forlorn
While victors swill their ale.

On Parliaments perches
Vultures sit,
They fight
And mix with crows,
Fly circling from misty pyres,
To pick the heads of foes.

How equally fierce
They love and fight.
Teach to heal and kill.
The wounded hero,
Loved by men.
They glory in his skill.

Embers of agony,
Harshest of pain.
Elite killers beg and howl,
Those who sent them
Burn and scream.
Death stares and wears a scowl.

Eva Kenton

SNOWBALL

Sometimes it snows
But not the way it used to.
Instead of clouds
It snows from plastic pouches,
Flows from silver foil
Into delicate piles,
Horizontal furrows,
Illusionary,
Invaluable soil.
Sculpted,
Shaped by the razor,
The knife,
The credit card.
Sucked into nasal tubes
With not even a sneeze.
Then!
Receding shyness,
Anxiety in discard
With the utmost ease.
Whilst the bitter nectar
Slowly trickling,
Glides the rear nasal.
Climbing backwards
Down the talking throat.
She says,
"Why is everyone an idiot?
Where my coat?"

Sometimes it snows
But not how it's supposed to.
It snows behind doors,
Then quickly goes.
Because it's harvested you see,
Tested and tried,
Through the innards of a blue note,
Bought and supplied.
A flurry of snow
Whizzing past her majesty's head,
Nasally vacuumed,
One squeezed, one flared.
The veracious ego
Unnaturally fed,
I know it sounds like farce.
Why does she do it?
She says, "Feels good, why not?
Everyone's talking rubbish.
Where my coat?"

Sometimes it snows
But not how it should.
It snows then leaves
Into awkward places,
Below windowless eyes
Into expectant faces.
The hose from the nose,
The sweeping snort,
Inhaling Charley,
Discretely bought.

The good gear,
Height of conversation,
"Charmed, I'm sure."
Charisma on turbo,
Soon need some more,
Personality float.
"There's a dealer.
Got to score.
HOW MUCH?
What a rip off,
Where's my coat?"

Sometimes it snows
And it is getting colder,
Or is it her getting older.
Not as young as she used to be,
Stress free.
Prozac and depression
Must run in the family!?
Not as quick as she used to be,
Used to be a runner you know,
Yeah, really!
She asks,
"Would you like a line?
Cause lines make rhymes.
And I'm feeling fine".
My inner voice says
"Spiritual theft?
The soul concealed?
Hide and seek?

Bereft"!
She says
"It's a part of her journey,
And we're all missing the boat.
Where has everybody gone?
Why has everybody left?
Where is my coat?"

Mervin Telford

GAMER

I've got my game on
Jacked in, high five,
Boredom buster,
Cranial overdrive.
I've got my game on
Move out the way.
The Force is with me,
I happily slay.
I've got my game on
My kids wonder why?
Bellies hungry,
Begin to cry.

I've got my game on,
Wife's alone again,
Stifled anger
"She's going insane".
I've got my game on
I'm alone at last,
My friend is the game,
I'm part of the cast.
My cheeks pale-hollow,
Thumbs hard and sore,
Encaged seclusion,
Love shines no more.
I've got my game on, why?

Mervin Telford

BEACON

In cotton landscapes
Dreamed a child,
In ethereal slumber
Held so mild.
It feared the dark
In an awakened state,
So a torch was gifted
By guardians great.
From triangular pillars
It lit the way
And rainbow playgrounds
It did display.

Under moonlit skies
The child awoke,
Took the torch and
Asunder broke.
"To see its inner parts!"
It spoke,
"To know its works
I must devise,
To take apart
And theorise?"

A scientist now
From sapling grown.
The being became
A tree well known.
The torches parts
Were laid to store.
To fit them back
They could no more.
Disdain surrounds
The being this day,
Destroyed the gift
That lit the way.

(Please see "Re – Ignited" page 134)

THE BARBER SHOP

Barber Naki,
Cool and easy.
Conductor of the oral word wizard's art.
Composer of the verbal symphony.
The day's lessons are about to start
His combs and cutters
Are cleaned and sharpened,
He lubricates his thoughts
With the "I am that I am"
Hones his mind with Aristotle.
Seeking the spirit that governs the man.

The shop is alive
With the sound of the barber's parable.
Hypnotic.
Laced with gesture and mime.
Hypothetical,
The ongoing mother of all stories.
Dishevelled realism made sublime.
Yesterday's memories translated to story.
Rearranged into lessons,
Food for the soul.
Spiritual manna
Freed from multiple experiences.
Reorganised just for that goal.

Afro hairs fall gracefully
Dark snowflakes.

Vibrating trimmer gliding,
On dark and caramel skin.
Snip, snaps of the scissors sculpting.
Respectful client
Warm comfort within.
The angled hand held mirror.
The gleeful look.
Action,
Reaction,
Appreciation.
The elusive discovery transparent.
The transience of the ego's elation.

The Barber stands quiet and listens,
Verbal Rat-tat-tat-tats
Arouse the air.
From teams of awaiting clientele,
Opposing views
Evoke wit and more flair.
Poison tipped,
Automatic,
Alphabetical arrows,
Ominous satire.
Entrenched views,
Emotional and bold.
Competing international opinions,
To tell the story that's never been told.
The lure of the "knock out" punch line.
Words fly like athletes
Unleashed from their blocks.

The true winner?
The multidimensional lyricist.
The omnipresent Barber's
Superior rhyme.

Recountable, emotional, hysterical tragedy.
Elongated memoirs.
Rib tickling comedy at an unstoppable pace.
Resurrectable tear filled laughter.
The broad smile on the listeners face.
For barber has become father and mother,
To those that sit in his chair.
Wisdom received and inspected,
His understanding permeates the air.
More knowledge unfolds before sister and brother.
Their subconscious graciously opens its doors.
The key?
The psychiatric head lock.
For mastery works on transmutable flaws.
Released, refined unilateral vision.
From the Barbers subliminal ray.
From the force of the time-delayed breakthrough,
The magical wish is here to stay.
The love of the eternal parents.
The disciple's strength
Reclaimed and re-bought.
The ring of the bell of Naki's Baba's shop.
Where knowledge is both gifted and sought.

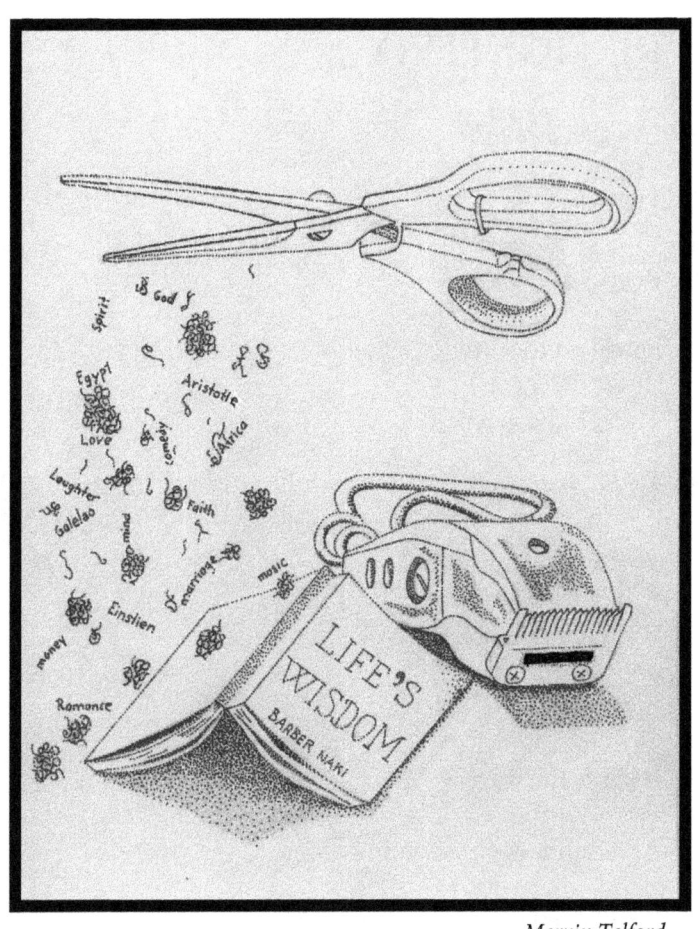

Mervin Telford

RE - IGNITED

"Awake, awake",

They sleep no more.

Retrieved the torch

Long laid to store.

The mind has served

To fit the parts.

The torch ignites

With faith filled hearts.

A flame again

It lights the way

And rainbow playgrounds

It will display.

VENOM OF CHANGE
5th key

Penetrating light.
Bright lasers
Into silken tissue sink.
Cellular change
Exact and foreboding.
Iced venom
To make us think.
In freedoms engine
Burns a vascular fire.
Holographic mindsets
Shrugged off in a blink.
These stages sent to test us.
Hollow Illusions
That push to the brink.

What fuels us to sacrifice
Our essence?
The energy of life
Attached to blood.
Consciously
Exchanging the dreams
Of the dreamer
For a transient monetary flood.
Personal wants,
Designs and sketches,
Trances and rhythms,
Melodious chants.

All are clarity shattered
By the souls' ascending dance.

The sight of sound
White light is revealing.
The watchers hammer
Strikes again and again.
Lethargy is torn and broken
Spirit enveloped and
Connected to flame.
Self-indulgence spilled
Onto burning ego.
Evaporating,
All twisted and strange.
Love has propelled
This age-old prediction.
This metamorphic
Venom of change.

Mervin Telford

ACQUISITION
4th key

With wings so slowly eroding,
This glutinous paste,
It clings.
The puppets' skyward strings reach
With thoughts attached to things.
Minds led and ridden by drunkards,
Remote controlled and high on things.
Dictated to, hoodwinked and commanded,
Lured, seduced and enamoured with things.

Life's adhesive
The concrete that binds us
And blinds our minds, these things.
For to have nothing is forbidden.
To be free of a thing is sin?
Communities spun, confused and reeling,
Mentally enslaved with countless things.
The need to win to be seen and successful, the goal?
The acquisition of multiple things.

Things separate kings from paupers.
The rich above the poor,
Yet all want more elation
With a thirst for more of those things.
We are told to seek, to need them,
So we work for more of these things.
Write lists of things to relieve us

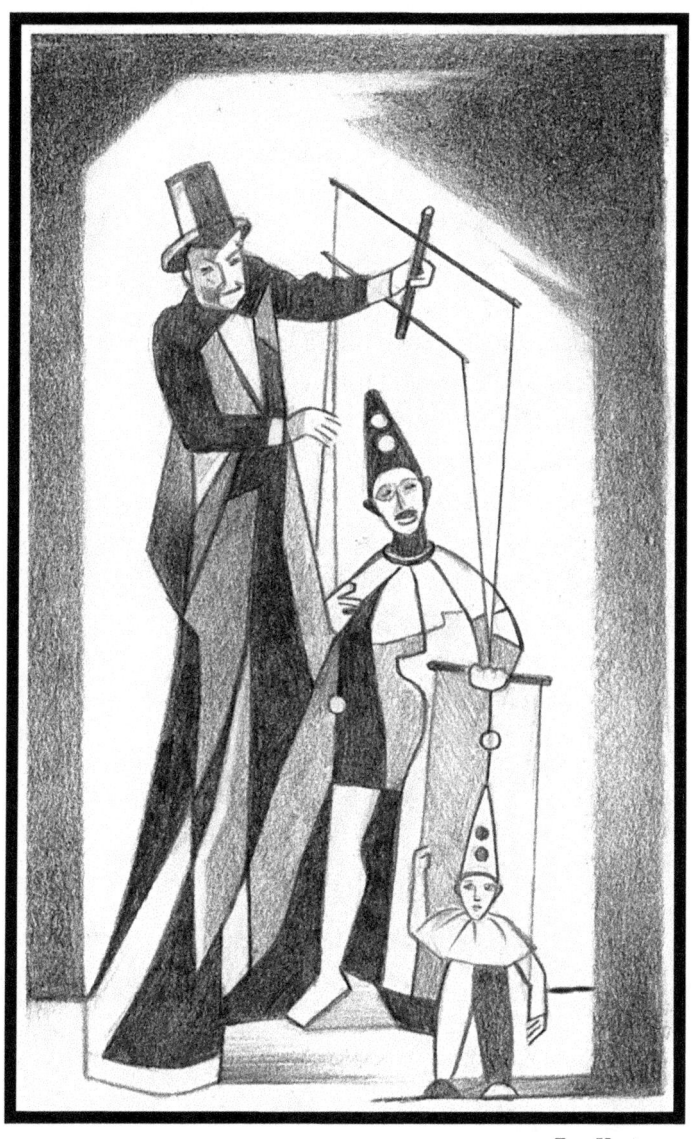

Eva Kenton

So that happiness is shaped by things.
To add value to life we chase them,
We run screaming when losing our things.
We commiserate death with sharing,
More old and worn out things.

We celebrate new life with buying,
Our dreams are swamped with things.
Our woes are eased with holding
More new and temporal things.
The challenge comes with no thing!
A mind with no attachments
Rises from the cave and sings.
A freedom thrust upon us,
A new dawn a new face brings.
So who are we with no thing?
With the question a new phase begins.
Utopia patiently awaits us
The price of admission?
To bring no things

ILLUSION'S KEY
An answered riddle

In this existence
Of 3D
You need me
For you to see.
For I am me
And you are thee.
Yet when we face
We are not free.
We are as one,
For you will always
In me be.
For without me
There is no you.
You say,
"It's imaginary"
Well, lets see.
Even with closed eyes
You see you through me.
For the image you hold of you
Would surely without me not be.
I am sought by all
Once bought no fee,
I am the ultimate grooming key.
Who am I?

I am illusions child
Called "reflection",
Irresistible, that's me.
Through mirrors
And cameras,
In retinal images I come,
That makes you and I as one.
And if your image is broken,
Bad luck,
"Seven years"
Is illusions decree.
So you see,
You need me
Even for you to be,
Lucky?
Deceptive master,
I am illusion's key.
If you leave
The world hologram
I will still be me.
Question!
Residual image?
Without me?
Who is it
That you will be?

Eva Kenton

BORN

Gasp!
Broken waters are flowing.
A new face
From discomfort is born.
Fired Into bright light
Innocence staring.
Gift wrapped
In a tiny form.

A mother's, father's prayer's
Have gently unfolded.
Tears with smiles on.
Flowers and curly lips.
Heartfelt,
Warm congratulations.
From youth's fountain
Time is gently eclipsed.

MAHOGANY CRADLE

Mahogany cradle,
Soft nest of love.
My head in repose,
Graceful smiles from above.

Mahogany cradle,
Under emerald eyes.
Through silk-filled clouds
Our spirit flies.

Mahogany cradle,
Fragrant, gentle and deep.
Warm and surrounded,
Awakened from sleep.

Mahogany cradle,
Under stratum skies.
Sheltered from rainfall,
Nurturing,
Tender surprise.

LOVE DANCE

Like the soft light of a new dawn
Breaking over a field of Arabian spices,
You are fragrant.
Charged with subtle flowing energies,
You are like heavenly children,
Joyfully playing in colour filled winds
To melodies not yet heard by mortal ears.

You are like sublime notes,
Played by ethereal instruments,
Caught in the ever-changing current of life.
Holding you is like dancing with an angel,
Like touching the wind,
Like gently caressing silk
With a feather light touch.

You are spiritual strength and beauty
Born of pain in life and love.
You are the healer come to be healed,
The giver come to receive.
You are born to be loved,
Are caught in a beam of love,
And emanate love untryingly.
You are a lifetime of silent prayers
Answered in an exquisite waking dream.

You are the sun
That brings the seed to bear its golden fruit.
You are all these things and much more.
To know you is to truly cherish the moment.

THE PLEDGE

Joy,
Elation,
Flowering creation,
Love rises,
Igniting,
Serenity released.
It graces the air,
Floats in on elation,
Embracing with freedom,
Its divinity's high priest

He stands smiling,
Heart tender with age.
She stands rejoicing,
On her beautiful stage.
Their words are building
And growing,
It's a wonderful display.
They pledge
Love eternally,
Verbally caressed,
Trembling,
Exhilarated this day.

His eyes warm
And tender,
Jubilant,
The family rejoice.

She shivers, blissfully
Beholding her choice.
Hand outstretched
His loving arms surround.
Their true love glows
And shines all around

Mothers smile in tears.
A blissful family today.
Faith has released its harvest
A wonderful display.
Pledges heard with feeling.
Joy and laughter abounds.
Food, enlivening Music,
Dancing to rhythmic sounds.
All have come to celebrate
The pledge of respect.
This resplendent union
Their love will reflect.

BAKERS' SACRAMENT

This mix is kneaded
With delicate skill,
As vibrant souls glide
The beckoning will.
Inner ease caresses,
Causing
The heart to bestow,
Energies are forming
A radiant dough.

Shining, bright
From head and jaw,
Words, trickling
Bright powder,
Knowledge rising
Ever more.
The magic of truth?
The bakers' sieve,
Inner prayer,
True friends arrayed,
With pure bread to share.

Dispensing,
Nourishment,
Giving food,
We are fed.
Souls receptive,
Baking,
Sacramental bread.
Watered and nurtured.

In magnificent bloom,
Students with smiles on,
In the Bakers' school room.

Supple minds looking forward,
Expectant and keen.
Loaves rising,
The sun's fire,
A heart warming scene.
Aromatic and shimmering,
All in good time.
Our bakers take materials
And make them sublime.
The permeating essence,
Fragrant, heady and fine.
The loaves' are all connected,
Their offerings refined.

Birthed are our dreams,
Friends are in full flight.
A luminous halo
Is drawn near
By our light.
Magic and ecstatic,
Hearts floating and minds free,
This permeating beauty,
A visual melody.
In sun light you'll see us,
The baker's sacrament we
Embrace.
The Grand baker ever watching
And smiling with grace.

YOU LOVE ME

You are iridescent Sovereign,
I am royal hue.
You are Mother, Father,
I am body, sky and stars.
You are the infinite garden.
In You I dream and grow
And You love me.

You are the eternal breath,
I am spirit exhaled.
You are purest essence,
I am the rugged trail.
You are the unfathomable Playwright,
I embellish with laughter and tears,
And You love me.

You are the life giving sun
And I the dancing fire.
You are the nurturing heart,
I am the warm cradle.
You are the word divine,
Through speech I bear your children
And still You love me.

You are the turquoise seas,
And I the mercy full soil.
You are infinite beginning,
I am the ongoing end.
You are the colour filled horizon
Within which I am gently embraced
And You will always love me.

GOLDEN CHALICE

Gentle heart,

Golden chalice

My soul mate.

Warm words

Genuine soul

Dreams merge.

Entwined energy

Inner knowing

I need you.

Importance growing

Accepted flaws,

Souls converge

Mervin Telford

SMALL AXE BIG TREE

There was a tree of high degree
That stood out from them all.
As I cast my eye over the array of trees
It looked brighter, large and tall.
I was perplexed by the beauty of this One tree.
Why was it different from the rest?
Had it been singled out and nurtured?
Had it been given natures best?

Curiosity overcame me,
I descended closer to see.
As our hearts embraced,
We connected,
Said the tree, "I'll soon be free".
Below the plentiful green foliage
Lurked a powerful choking vine,
Said the vine "the foliage that you see
Is altogether mine".
For it had drawn its energy
From the tree,
Becoming green, lush and sublime.
It had sought dominium over the tree
By slowly climbing and squeezing throughout time.

Mervin Telford

A few had passed to look and see,
But none had seen the hidden vine.
They thought the tree was healthy
And always in its prime.
Together we pulled at
The mighty vine.
We sliced, untangled and we pried.
Said the tree
"I have done what all trees do,
I have nourished and supplied.
The vine was doing what it knows best
To cling, dominate, suckle and grow.
As a tree I have stood the test of time
And onwards I will go".
In unison we overcame the
Powerful strangling vine;
The tree stands glorious to this day.
And now we go to set others free
Against all odds come what may.

ALIVE

Great Spirit

Who are you?

How do you dream?

Weaving together the

Lives of the named

Married into the infinite void.

Love us now

And remember this,

Our matrimonial bond.

Here with you,

Alive,

We are alive.

Eva Kenton

EDEN'S CHILDREN
SERIES 5
EARLY EPISODES

The messenger brought me to
The ethers in earth's outer atmosphere.
I was taken back to a time when
Ancient Vimana's navigated her skies.
I saw the scaled ones and how they
Mined her mineral rich lands.
I saw the lifeblood of the elder race,
Tested, twisted and fused,
And witnessed the birthing of
Eden's children.
I watched and was frightened
As the "negatives" put on cloaks,
Disguising themselves as mentors,
Self proclaimed Gods of light.
I saw them secretly feast
On the flesh and blood
Of the innocent.

I saw enlightened men and women
Walk amongst the spellbound.
Saying, unveiling and teaching,
Feeding the hungry with their words.
They were slain for their sharing.
I stared in disbelief as empires rose.
Giants marched within armies.
Blood fought against blood.

Fuelled by injected lies.
Subterfuge enriching the elite.
I was shown how wars
Create vortices of negative energy,
Energy used to succour the cabal.
Continually, battles raged
Until there was little left
But plumes of smoke
Around broken bodies.
I painfully watched as
Stooped and shivering mothers
Shed tears into the wet red sands.
As I watched
I too shed tears.

ELIXIR'S CHILDREN
FUTURE EPISODES

Taken forward in time
I looked in wonder at how
Earth had been transformed.
I saw a queen amongst queens,
Glorious beyond words,
A calm and noble, sentient planet.
I marvelled at her heavenly
Paradisiacal lands,
At her vibrant lakes,
Rivers and oceans,
Teaming with life.
Her bounteous natural foods
Fed all.

Birds of beauty flew in her skies,
All creatures grew from her
And became honoured by her.
I saw children playing
With former beasts of prey,
All running freely,
Inhaling her fragrant breath.
Happy and grateful.
Rejoicing at her mercy,
Her justice and her love.
I saw men and women communing
With spirit once again.
Receiving guidance and council
From Creation's unseen worlds.

All gloried in their new wisdom.
I watched all of this
And wept again
But this time with joy.

Eva Kenton

SLEEP & MEDITATION, THE SILENT ORACLES
4th Key

Through you are eons of wisdom
No more scattered and concealed.
You irrigate our hopes and ideals.
Our loves and desires are by you revealed.
And when we slumber in your arms,
That for which we long for
Is weighed within the
Softness of your breasts,
And tested in dreams
With thrills and charms.

You are the sweet pillow
That gives comfort,
And cushions against the rock.
You are the womb
That cradles our tender hearts,
Nurturing against the storms
Of life's cruel clock.
Oh, but the fruits of one night with you
Gives more comfort
Than a myriad of silken days of
You bereft.
One night without you
Is one that blights our view.

Eva Kenton

You sooth our flesh
And fly with our Spirits unbound.
You are the oracle that all life seeks.
All creatures know your song.
And when we are held
In your delicate wings
Mortality is but a distant kiss from a
Mouth that never speaks.
And when you are gone
Your melody of signs linger,
Guiding all to their forgotten wishes
And where they most belong.

"GUIDE OF SOULS"

"I am that I am"
I seek not to attain perfection
In the eyes of man.
It is enough that I do my best.
Life and the universe is
Ever evolving and changing,
Therefore I am unfinished.
In my gardens I cultivate love,
 Courage, faith and determination;
And the pursuit of knowledge through
Learning, experience, challenge and resistance.
Succession and change is ongoing.
Growth is attained by this medium.
Manifested change leads to a dimensional shift
That gives to each their own.
I look to see an approach to this
Change with hope, faith, courage
And a noble heart.
I strive to make a difference,
Be it through direct positive action or
Through adversity in experience in this
Your perfectly imperfect world.
I look at this illusionary plane with satisfaction,
For it is a means to an end.
It is a vehicle toward self-knowledge and Godhood.

I am content at what was,
Do not dote on what should have been.
All time is linked and bound,
Yet limitless, for I am that I am,
Bending time around.
I seek to endow my thoughts,
Words and actions with passion.
Sometimes silent, gentle, tamed,
Sometimes wild, noisy, untamed.
My stories although often strange,
Have hidden meaning,
Meant for the inner eyes and inner ears.
Sometimes I play advocate through chaos,
For often it is the only path to clarity, for I am that I am.
I am courageous in well timed forward movement,
I am undaunted by seamless stillness and silence.
I permeate the so called "positive and negative",
Yet I love and am loved.
Never lingering too long in the stagnation of the past.
I exercise my right to change
My mind, my appearance and direction within
The ebb and flow of the grand tapestry.
Fleeting though it may seem,
Positive mind-fire engages with causality
And ignites creativity through love and passion.
Projected energy and the continuity of intention
Leads to the magic of manifestation and change.

Through this medium I am often misunderstood
And feared among the misinformed,
Yet, in the aftermath of paradigm shifts
I am honoured or revered.
I am love and am eternally redefined by
The expressions of my creations.
From their hearts of hearts.
"I am that I am"
"Guide of souls"

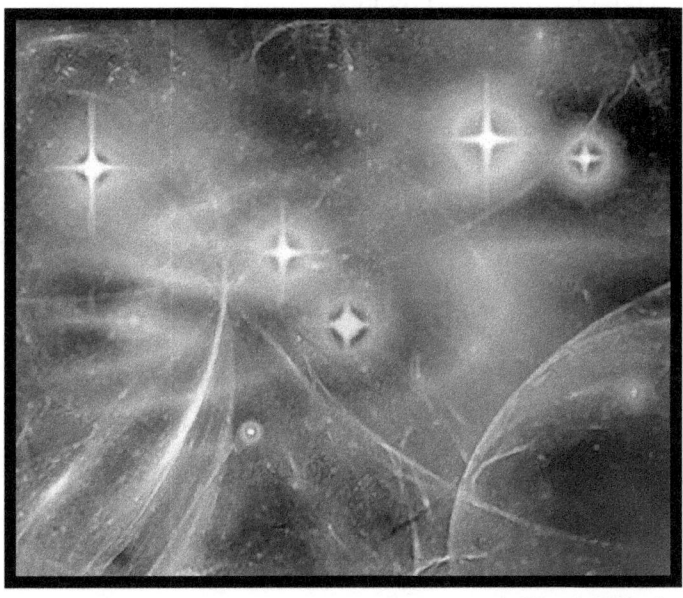

Mervin Telford

HEROES

Shall we not accept what is given and rise?

We rise,

Afraid, unafraid,

Travelling the heroes' path.

Into the deep.

Deeper into the mystery,

Unfolding journey into bliss.

Fire of the heart.

This,

Only this is real.

Eva Kenton

THE ASCENDANCY
7th key

As I am flown from home
Pre-existent memories stayed,
And I,
Delivered aeronautically,
Breath in this new facade.
I have come with multiple others
With a directive to ease,
The physical senses tutored,
Gently guiding the trustees.
An unquenchable thirst for the exquisite,
With humility as a guide.
All giving and creating,
Gethsemane applied.

Especially amongst the wealthy
Poverty's talon prevails,
But the naked eye sees nothing,
True senses discern misleading trails.
Metamorphosis is upon us:
The catalyst?
Truth and pain.
The challenge of the forger's hammer
Accepted again and again.
Pride dismantled through discomfort,
Fear offered to the light with ease,
Intimidation turned to supplication,
Humbled supplicants on strong knees.

Of those who come to the ascendancy
Many will choose Horus' eye.
Clinging to material remembrances
As the summit beckons them
Heaven high.
They reach for bulbous wallets
To purchase stronger limbs,
With a lust for physical comfort,
They fly with borrowed wings.
Wearily and expectant
They sit and cross their legs,
As taught and straining porters
Lift their load and shake their heads.

Heaving ever upward
Nebulous fat hung
From a weight bent pole,
The labourers are undaunted
As the arduous journey takes its toll.
A sword, denied the forger's hammer,
Breaks before the real battle has begun.
The weight compacts the spine
Of the bearer
As he climbs towards the sun.

Weak with child,
Pale, drawn and hungry,
A woman begins her courageous climb.
Love has touched her forehead,
The mystery of what is

Has been made sublime.
Her flesh yields to the warm comfort
Of the guide from the mists of time.
Her faith unfolds its power,
Her countenance begins to shine.
I see her smiling on the summit
At the place of splendour upon high.
We awe at the surrounding beauty,
It draws a peaceful sigh.
The steps have born their harvest,
Even to those with borrowed wings.
In every heart is a map of promise
To where celestial joy begins.

Eva Kenton

THE SCULPTOR
1st Key

In the beginning was the Void,
And the Void decreed,
"Let there be Intention,
And agreement and retention.
Thereby let nothing be destroyed".
And as it was decreed,
So there was fission,
And so Intention was deployed.

Intention declared,
"Let there be Imagination and elation,
Let all imagery have relation".
And as it was intended,
So it became.
Thus Imagination came to fame.

Imagination thought,
"Let there be Creation and recreation,
Let all resonant substance
Have its station".
And as it was imagined,
So it appeared.
Thus Creation became revered.

Creation said,
"Let there be geometry
With sound and sight".
And as it was crafted,
So it became.

And there came structure
And melody and light,
And all was pure and resonant and bright.

Soon an image came to Imagination
By Intention,
And was given to Creation
To be allotted its given station.
And Creation gave it form,
Thus was a living sculpture born.

With Intention and Imagination,
Creation agreed to give it breath,
Thereby saving it from death.
And the sculpture was given a name,
It was called "Hu-man, Eternal Flame".
And there historically it stood,
For all to see
That it was good.

Mervin Telford

LETTER TO THE DEPARTED

When you left
Unexpectedly
I sobbed.
Indifference vanquished
In my sudden loneliness.
Uncontrollably
I wept for all the times
That I should have but didn't.
Emotions, rising and dipping
Through a haze of tears.

As the years pass
I cherish your invisible energy
That is felt even from afar.
Your comedy,
Your love, your wisdom,
Your words of assurance
Echo in the universe of my mind,
Resonating delicately
In the robust chambers of my heart.

You have gone,
Yet you are still with me.
For I am
Of your flesh,
Of your mind,
Of your soul.
Continuing your legacy
Of awakening,

Transformation,
Metamorphosis.
For I am
Your child.

Eva Kenton

WISDOM COMES QUIETLY
6th key

Wisdom comes quietly,

In silence it unfolds,

Quenching the fires of the world.

In tears it leaves bookmarks,

So we can read and re-read,

And in so doing eventually understand.

In laughter it gives a promise

To the children of tomorrow.

Its feathered wings

Bear the heavy load,

And when we surrender

To the illusion of time,

Wisdom comes beautifully

And quietly.

Eva Kenton

AFTERWARDS

When I am gone

Plant the best of me in your gardens,

I will not grow

But I will nourish all that is there.

After my departure

Cast fond memories of me

Into sunlit southern winds

That they may fly unhindered

Bringing warmth into your dreams.

While I travel

Sing a song for me in your hearts

That I may know your melody

And attribute a clear voice to your soul.

Embellish my journey with love

And sweet fragrances,

They will help guide my senses

To help prepare your golden havens.

Mervin Telford

WE ANGELS

This initiation,

This pre-ordained creation

Illumined to a newer creed

With a persistent hammering,

Negating greed.

We, with a disciplined heart,

A new combined focus,

Re-defined soul and

A clear evolutionary chart,

With visualisation training

We transmute sin,

Forge the sight

And focus to win.

We study the masters

And their imperative techniques.

They say

"To hone the mind

Is to hone the auric physique"

We disciples are taught

To direct the rays.

The will of iron to emanate
The blinding light of love
That sears the gaze,
And reconstitutes the mind
From the confuser of ways.
We Angels descend,
Sent to defend.
To help ascend,
To protect and heal
From negative thought
And life's blows of steel.
We guide the neophyte
To the temple door.
Vanquishing
Principalities and powers,
We fear no more.
The unsuspecting traveller
Enters the demon's domain,
Dispersed with light
We remove disdain.
From clouds of anger
To hoards of hate

We protect the lonely traveller

At the pilgrims gate.

We forge our will,

As Angels.

Mervin Telford

THE BATTLE

Prime directed

Through the time gate's flight

The vortex brings the arena to sight,

Where unseen legions descend

On mortals to scheme.

Feeding entities,

We have come to clean.

Demons lead them,

Hissing and howling.

Apparition filled skies.

Against this opponent

We assail with surprise.

The warrior rises.

Shocked,

They are nullified by will.

Quantum Radiation,

Directed with skill.

Evasive and struggling

We corral our foes.

The nets are twisting and writhing

Mervin Telford

We go to dispose.

So that Earths loved havens

Can again breathe in repose.

As for our angel friends

Who courageously fought,

Deeds are weighed and balanced

With the utmost thought.

Their reward?

The Angels' soul yields,

They feel the rejuvenating breeze

Of the Elixir Fields.

We forge our will

As guardian angels.

THE GOOD NEWS

Sshshh, do you see it?
Something is very special!
And within sight.
We the collective
With lighter hearts
See truths freed
And in full flight.
Propagating humility,
Courage agendas
And new life speeches,
Re-told and bright.
Awakened energies,
Life giving affirmations,
Securing inner warmth.
New built bridges
Give rise to more answers.
The master dispenser
Reaches,
And teaches to
Love all who are sent.
A noble road!
Who are they?
What do they look like?
We say "all who can hear,
See or touch, of any colour",
The master's code.
Lived with intent.
And who is most masterful?
The" I am all"
And his word has spread,
Ask the hallowed man.

The people are joyous.
Mass awakened.
Security restored and
Global empathy is now enjoyed,
And all artists are employed.
"Freedom of speech is abundant".
Truth enjoyed means
The colour on the brush is
Deployed and vibrant.
Painting exhilarating scenes
On canvases,
Gloriously arrayed and recumbent.

People growing in the winds,
Like ascending trees.
While gardeners feed the planet
And everyone believes.

Sshshh, quiet,
Do you hear it?
Something sounds beautiful,
Exchanged,
Changed.
Our people are with song,
Exuding and growing,
Immunity strengthened,
DNA re-arranged,
Self governing,
Self realising,
And showing.
Soothing with new riches,
Earths children are re-born.
Healing,
Glad hearts yielding,
Faces smiling.

The good news
Taught with truth and feeling.
Freed spirits are flying,
Saved and healed.
We are harvesting new crops,
And are giving freely,
A mighty yield, no more buying.
Leaner, faster and stronger,
Faces are radiant.
Giving with love, applying.
The warming fruits of
The great harvest supplying,
Plentiful,
My people with joy are crying.

People, growing in the winds
Like ascending trees.
While gardeners feed the planet
And everyone believes.

Shhhshh, quiet.
Do you smell it?
Breathe,
Something is sweet!
Warm and scented,
Senses made keen,
The fragrant ground walked on
With perfumed, fresh feet.
Togetherness, peace,
And understanding,
Wisdom expanding!
Room for thought and cause,
Serendipity,
A blank sheet,
New children safe and playing.

Ideas and epiphanies
Triggered by more truths
And realised universal laws.
Organic and with comfort
New clothes
For new souls
Bringing "unite and live" manifestos,
United agenda,
Utilitarianism magnifying
A healed planet.
Yielding healing balms.
A healed and healthy people
With wholesome ecologies.
New oracles,
Love,
Light
Aesthetics,
And unity games.
Means
Fully cognisant young
With internal dreams,
Externally projected,
Mental premonitions,
Utopian prophecies realised.
The wise man walks
And talks again.
Human heights means
Self propelled flights made easier

People, growing in the winds
Like ascending trees.
While gardeners feed the planet
And everyone believes.

(PTO)

Shhshh, do you feel it?
Something very right
Celebrations.
Seeds, nuts, grains and
Exotic fruits,
Vegetables shinning,
Colourful and live.
Dancing with visible riches.
A transaction made with love.
Utopia,
Land of milk and honey.
Realised formula,
Tried and tested,
Natural and work invested.
Golden wings of freedom.
People creating and happy.
Drinking a new Elixir,
A relish and a wonder.
An ode to honesty.
The time-delayed dream,
The light,
The night
And the peaceful slumber.
Advert for a dream weaver,
Leading to comfort, inhaling.
Exhaling magnetised love.
Sending gifts like falling stars
And every store is an open
Energy giver.

To replenish evermore
The minds river.
The present is loaded
We have remembered
It is the collective that helps us deliver.

People, growing in the winds
Like ascending trees.
While gardeners feed the planet
And everyone believes.

Eva Kenton

TO AIDN I CAME

To Aidn I came.
Today I saw things
That will always allow me to
Appreciate comfort and ease...

I saw volunteers
Healers of men.
Standing knees merged
With light filled liquid,
Further enriching
Beautiful garments.
With Fragrant,
Perfumed essences.
Delivered by skilled,
Caring hands,
Gently caressing and purifying cloaks
With smooth, moist ether of alabaster.
Over and over.
Glowing and love infused.
Ready for the wearer.
Hour after hour,
Day after day,
Re-igniting,
Re-defining
Re-Energising.

To Aidn I came...
Today I saw things
That will always allow me to
Appreciate comfort and ease.

I saw gifted children
Realise their talents and inner wealth.
Tiny hands
Raised in thanksgiving and praise.
A Playful nudge and pull at a sleeve.
A teacher's tender advice.
A confident child,
Asking,
Requesting an assignment.
Smiling thereafter.
Understanding and patient.
An Elixian seer walks amongst us.
His shimmering garments
Slowly Swissshhh against the marble floor
His crystal like eyes look skyward,
As if in silent prayer,
"I am all, THAT I am, I am all, THAT I am"
Is chanted by his soft, strong voice,
A voice made audible
By a reverent silence.
All smile inwardly
At the familiarity and meaning
Of his words.

To Aidn I came.
Today I saw things
That will always allow me to
Appreciate comfort and ease...

Divinity moves gracefully
Weaving through the crowd.
I look again closely.

I see strong, supple peoples,
Powerfully jointed,
Reinforced with light:
This is Divinity
Alive within man,
Remade and reformed.
He walks on higher levels of being,
Giving as he does so.
Continually passed,
Seen by the crowd,
Each into another's eyes.
There they see the Devine.
Long ago infused,
Sensitised by those with stronger limbs
The seers of old.
The healed ones,
Who recognised the children of the fruitful,
With healing hearts as gifts.
Their emblem of revival.

To Aidn I came.
Today I saw things
That will always allow me to
Appreciate comfort and ease.

IN A PLACE WHERE

ALL CAN SUDDENLY

SEE

THE ONE EYED

MASTER BECOMES A

SERVANT TO ALL

A NEW PLANE

ELIXIR

A NEW NAME

TO BE CONTINUED

www.ingramcontent.com/pod-product-compliance
Lightning Source LLC
Chambersburg PA
CBHW071454040426
42444CB00008B/1336